INTEGRAL ECOLOGY
AND THE FULLNESS OF LIFE

D1526680

INTEGRAL ECOLOGY

and the

FULLNESS OF LIFE

Theological and
Philosophical Perspectives

ANTHONY J. KELLY

Paulist Press
New York / Mahwah, NJ

The poems, "Connections," on page 62, "Five Senses," on page 63, and "The Forest," on page 71 are from *Collected Poems (1942 to 1985)* by Judith Wright. Reprinted by permission of HarperCollins Publishers.

The Scripture quotations contained herein are from the New Revised Standard Version: Catholic Edition, Copyright © 1989 and 1993, by the Division of Christian Education of the National Council of the Churches of Christ in the United States of America. Used by permission. All rights reserved.

Cover image by graja/Shutterstock.com
Cover design by Joe Gallagher
Book design by Lynn Else

Library of Congress Cataloging-in-Publication Data
Names: Kelly, Anthony, 1938- author.
Title: Integral ecology and the fullness of life : theological and philosophical perspectives / Anthony J. Kelly.
Description: New York : Paulist Press, 2018. | Includes bibliographical references and index.
Identifiers: LCCN 2017052744 (print) | LCCN 2018016543 (ebook) | ISBN 9781587687419 (Ebook) | ISBN 9780809153688 (pbk. : alk. paper)
Subjects: LCSH: Human ecology—Religious aspects.—Catholic Church. | Ecotheology. | Catholic Church. Pope (2013- : Francis). Laudato si'. | Catholic Church—Doctrines.
Classification: LCC BX1795.H82 (ebook) | LCC BX1795.H82 K45 2018 (print) | DDC 261.8/8—dc23
LC record available at https://lccn.loc.gov/2017052744

ISBN 978-0-8091-5368-8 (paperback)
ISBN 978-1-58768-741-9 (e-book)

Published by Paulist Press
997 Macarthur Boulevard
Mahwah, New Jersey 07430

www.paulistpress.com

Printed and bound in the
United States of America

To my colleagues in the
Australian Catholic Theological Association

Contents

Introduction

ON PENTECOST SUNDAY, May 24, 2015, Pope Francis issued his encyclical letter on ecology and climate, titled *Laudato Si': On Care for Our Common Home* (*LS*). In terms of Catholic teaching and its dialogue with ecological sciences, as in the field of ecumenical and even interreligious collaboration and communication, it was a major event and continues to have steady influence.

My earlier book, *Laudato Si': Integral Ecology and the Catholic Vision*,[1] was largely a theological response to the encyclical. It teases out the implications of fundamental doctrinal and spiritual topics, most of which explicitly figure in *LS*. In this present work, we go further, not by concentrating on specific topics in the encyclical, but by suggesting more fully what an *integral ecology* implies— hence, the subtitle, *Theological and Philosophical Perspectives*. Ecology can hardly be "integral" if it ignores the transcendent source and end of our interrelational existence, or if it sets itself apart from the real being of the universe in which all things participate and exist in an interconnectedness and communion. What emerges is a widespread collaborative, not only on the part of the sciences and economics, but also those areas with a specifically human concentration such as anthropology, sociology, politics, and art, and more, since no area of knowledge or exploration—theology and philosophy, for instance—can be left out of the conversation. For all participants in such exchanges, this requires practicing a proper docility regarding the scientific analyses of the situation, and recognizing the authority of experts on such questions of climate change, desertification, ocean warming, common political approaches, and so on. Others can make their best contribution in terms of faith, theology, spirituality, morality, as well as a range of philosophical questions dealing with the distinctiveness of the human, the integral meaning of ecology, the phenomenon of human consciousness, and its place in the community of living things.

Ecological concerns can occasion serious levels of depression, disillusionment, and conflict. In the present critical period, the field of ecology can seem to many as a zone of irreconcilable conflicts in which no one ever learns or experiences an open-minded meeting with others. Hopefully, by evoking a larger and more philosophical dialogue, a genuinely integral ecology will emerge and avoid the danger of ideological divisiveness and monodimensional mindsets. Inevitably, there will be opposing points of view, even though there are new modes of collaboration to be discovered and more inclusive and respectful conversations to be conducted. An integral ecology holds the promise of a more authentic humanity. We are impelled to communicate at the onset of a "common era" of appreciation of the wonder and diversity of life on this planet.

Does this suggest that we are about to relapse into the dreaded anthropocentric mindset that assumed that only the human mattered, and all else in heaven and on earth was for the sake of our human well-being and progress? I think not. To appreciate the role and responsibility of the human within the "sublime communion" of life on planet Earth does not demean other forms of life in this biosphere, but it does point to quite a special mission of the human in "caring for our common home"—to quote the subtitle of Pope Francis's encyclical. The phenomenon of human consciousness, the human capacity to know, to respond, and to experience the wonder and beauty of life, necessarily casts us into the role of being pro-ecological agents. The emergence of the human brings a capacity to register meaning beyond sense impressions, to respond to value beyond instinctual attractions, and to awaken to moral consciousness. It means living beyond the confines of a mere habitat, entering an expanding world, and awakening as a participant in a boundless universe.

In that respect, there is a distinctiveness of the human that—

regardless of how much it shares a genetic inheritance with other animals—we must respect and defend. After all, there have been no reports so far of a pod of whales holding a conference on the declining quality of plankton, or of leopards gathering to plan a cosmetic makeover to change their spots, or of dolphins who, after meeting in prayer, have decided to assert the rights of fish. We have no information of any lemmings exploring less wasteful organizational procedures, or of the higher apes writing monographs on the meaning of life. Any developments in such directions have so far escaped detection. As a result, questions of meaning and value, of a universal sense of the totality and our responsibility within it, seem to be left to the human. With all other animals, the human being breathes the air of this planet; but human consciousness inhales the atmosphere of another realm—one that is original and ultimate.

From Aristotle on, previous generations spoke of the human as the "rational animal" (*zoon logikon* in Greek, *animal rationale* in Latin). This was the classic description of the human as the biophysical lifeform that can reflect on itself, and even reflect on its own reflecting. Through evolutionary biology, there is new understanding of the process in which human existence has emerged, with a rediscovery of the basic animality of the human. The human is not somehow circling the globe looking for a temporary physical habitation. Rather, the human animal shares with all other animals a common emergence and structure in a biophysical world, with needs, emotions, and the instincts to bond, reproduce, care for young, and so forth.

Yet there remains the "rational" aspect—that strange capacity in the human for thought and freedom. There is the capacity for reflective openness to everything—from the genetic makeup of our bodies and the brain's trillion neurons, to the phenomenon of consciousness itself—and all its manifestations in faith, science, philosophy, art—and this reflection on integral ecology. The connotations, first of all, are largely negative: integral ecology is not to be realized by excluding any domain or dimension of knowledge from consideration. In this regard, it envisages, however imperfectly, not only particular ecological niches, or even larger habitats, or even the whole terrestrial biosphere, but the incomprehensible totality of existence and life as registered in human consciousness.

It is to be received, as in Pope Francis's phrase, as a gift of "sublime communion" (*LS* 89).

Clearly, integral ecology does not begin from a ready-made synthesis; it is always in the making. From our experience of bodily consciousness emerge science and all scientific specializations. The manifold creativity of knowledge does not replace our immediate experience but articulates it.[2] An integral ecology can learn much from phenomenological works intent on disclosing the experience that is at "the heart of reason." Rather than take for granted the post-Enlightenment fragmentation of knowledge and the endless proliferation of specializations pointing us away from the concreteness of experience, it is better to be immersed in reality as it is given before any rational analysis, in ways that precede concepts, systems, or even verbal formulae. The *given* is that we consciously exist and coexist, immersed and participating in the inexpressible totality of the universe. An embodied participation in the universe is the precondition for all scientific and practical knowledge. Complex cultural and social conditions have tended to mute the revelatory power of religious and even philosophical language in their deepest registers of meaning, making a genuinely integral ecology impossible.

The current ecological crisis, however, calls for a new collaboration. What follows presents the horizon in which a new sense of conscious connections with the biosphere of this earth, the encompassing cosmic reality, and the singularity of Christian revelation might come to expression.

Chapter 1, "Toward an Integral Ecology," indicates the wide horizon of our investigation, as it is informed at every step by the contributions of those who have a particular expertise in the variety of fields and specializations. In this regard, an integral ecology must go beyond particular descriptions of earthly life to include an ecology of meaning. Here, the accent is on connections, interconnections, implications, and analogical linkages—a specific version of that "framework for collaborative creativity" commended by Bernard Lonergan's *Method in Theology*, and other writers who have emphasized the need for new forms of ecological collaboration today.

Chapter 2, "Contexts," includes the larger story of life on planet Earth. The very fact that we are earthlings existing and even coexisting within this particular universe surely suggests that we have something in common, and that collaboration for the well-being of the planet has become urgently imperative—hence, the value in continuing to explore versions of a common story of origins from different perspectives and the need for a new paradigm for a new age hospitable to the rigorous objectivity of the scientist, the creativity of the artist, and the unutterable experience of the mystic, and in the everyday patterns of communication and action in the daily life of the world.

Chapter 3, "Ecological Conduct," suggests that integral ecology is about becoming someone in mind, heart, and imagination, and doing something in action, as a participant in a global conversion. Here, we consider the value of various kinds of action, along with the role of the higher form of action that is contemplation: a mindful and heartfelt indwelling of the world. What does this mean for the language of our communication, and even the meaning of our humanity, with its unique capacity to ask the big questions arising from the world in which we live, the universe in which we participate with the character and capacity of the human? Here, we touch on the "inner ecology" of human consciousness as integral to the health of the biophysical ecology of terrestrial life.

Chapter 4, "Indwelling Creation," treats the realities of the Creator, creation, and ecology from the perspective of human consciousness, the better to interiorize our sense of the presence of God and to extend the possibility of dialogue on many fronts. Such an approach moves "from the inside out," with the emphasis on experience, the phenomenon of consciousness and intentionality. This contrasts with the perspective "from the outside in," with its concern for the purely objective, but which lacks an explicit focus on the interiority of the thinking, feeling, loving, and acting subject. Modern science has shown magnificence in its concentration on empirical data regarding the material constitution of the universe and the stages of evolution. It has, however, tended to neglect another kind of data, namely, the data of consciousness that enable human consciousness itself, along with science, ecology, and the life of the spirit, to be examined in a more ample and integrated fashion—in the interests of any integral ecology.

Chapter 5, "Christ and Integral Ecology," suggests that for an integral ecology, the meaning of the incarnation is crucial, but understood as an expanding event. The resurrection and ascension of Christ do not mean that he is disincarnate and disembodied, but, rather, that he is fully embodied in the world as it will ultimately be. It is not that the risen Christ is now disembodied, but that we human beings are not yet fully embodied in him within a transformed creation. The incarnation continues, and the world in which the Word was made flesh reaches, in Christ, an unimaginable fulfillment. What are the consequences for an integral ecology? We reflect on this question in chapter 7, "Ecology and Eschatology."

Chapter 6, "Befriending Death," acknowledges that there is little room for death in many presentations of ecology, even though death is an obvious ecological reality as generation follows generation. It has been remarked that a primal fear of death motivates so much of culture and individual lifestyles—and even ecology! The denial of death, therefore, has ecological consequences; as well, it calls into question the superficial ecology that is sustained merely by romantic optimism. By reflecting on the ecological significance of death, we can ensure that the framework of integral ecology will remain truly open to the witness of Christian faith and hope, and see more fully how the Christian vision of creation brings a special depth and hope into ecological concerns. Faith in Christ is an ever-renewable resource in a world of dwindling resources.

In chapter 7, we note how Pope Francis's *Laudato Si'* provokes the need for both an ecological and eschatological reflection on how ultimate fulfillment in Christ includes the liberation and transformation of earthly nature itself. Hope envisages the end when God will be "all in all" (1 Cor 15:28). The biblical perspectives presenting the city of God (see Rev 21:5) and the Lamb slain from the foundation of the world (see Rev 12:11) extend the range and concreteness of hope, along with a deeper appreciation of both the God-willed multiplicity of creation and the primordial creativity of love itself. The focus remains incarnational in that the Word not only became flesh but is also an "earthling" in a planetary environment. Consequently, eschatological fulfillment does not entail the abolition of the natural world, but its unimaginable fulfillment.

In chapter 8, "An Open-Ended Ecology," the mystical orientation of Christian faith is characterized by a *universal* and unrestricted scope. The range of faith surpasses the particularities of doctrinal, theological, or moral contexts. It breathes and "has been groaning" (Rom 8:18–28) in the mystery of the Holy Spirit, who inspires hopes for a wholeness that cannot be thought, imagined, or named. Such universality in the Spirit inspires the most radical form of catholicity as openness to the all, yet as waiting for what is not yet.[3] Faith, at its most radical point, dwells in a totality that no thought or system or action can express or achieve. It works more as a *reductio in mysterium* (Karl Rahner), as all things are brought back to the original and abiding mystery at work in everything and everyone. In that sense of universal mystery, we find an abiding dimension of integral ecology.

For Christians in the process of facing doctrinal and institutional differences, the sources of original unity and present healing emerge. Thus, the door is opened to the development of relationships and respectful but critical interactions of mutual enrichment, all in the interest of a healthy ecology in the specific life-form that is Christian existence. Furthermore, the love of God, at the heart of the gospel, not only brings the imperative to love one's neighbor, it also overflows into love of, and care for, the "neighborhood"—if the neighbor is to be truly loved, and if the Creator of all is to be truly honored.

Finally, just as despair is fundamentally a failure of imagination, real hope is formed out of the active imagination of those who have the humility to recognize this earth as the shared body of our existence. Imagination regains its courage when it is prepared to diagnose the harm caused by the refusal of our earthly status. More positively, creativity is newly inspired to the degree we give ourselves to a more intimate collaboration with the gracious mystery of Life, however it has been revealed to us.

CHAPTER 1

Toward an Integral Ecology

BEYOND *LAUDATO SI'*

ECOLOGY CAN HARDLY be "integral" if it ignores the universe of real being in all its interconnectedness, or refuses to consider the transcendent source and end of our existence. This entails a widespread collaborative effort, not only on the part of the sciences and economics, but also including all the human concerns that are the domain of anthropology, sociology, politics, art, and more—since no one can be left out of the conversation. For theologians, as noted earlier, this requires a proper docility regarding scientific analyses, and leaving to experts such questions of climate change, desertification, ocean warming, and the like, while at the same time making our best contribution in terms of faith, theology, spirituality, and certain philosophical questions.

In a world of dwindling resources, it is good to stress the necessity of the ever-renewable resources of Christian faith and hope. As discussed earlier, ecological concerns can occasion serious levels of depression and disillusionment, unless such ecology is truly "integral" in allowing for the spiritual resources that can come from religious faith. Faith may not provide a detailed program, let alone additional information, but it does inspire hope and a sense of living in an environment in which the Word became flesh, and in a universe called into existence by God's creative love. By evoking this larger religious horizon, the danger of ideological divisiveness and monodimensional mindsets might be avoided.

Ecology is a serious business, and those involved—either theoretically or practically—know the stress of contradiction and opposition. A genuinely integral ecology works in the largest possible horizon while being informed at every step by the contributions of those who have a particular expertise. There inevitably will be opposing points of view, even though there are new modes of collaboration to be discovered and more inclusive and respectful conversations to be conducted in a "cosmopolis" of ecological concern.[1] More generally, history can progress only through a consistent exercise of collaboration and self-transcendence in the cosmopolis that Lonergan describes. Only when individual and group bias is held in check and the way opened to genuine self-transcendence and the pursuit of what is truly good for all, can history get beyond the pursuit of individual social and even national self-interest. He writes,

> What is necessary is a cosmopolis that is neither class nor state, that stands above all their claims, that cuts them down to size, that is founded on the native detachment and disinterestedness of every intelligence, that commands man's first allegiance, that implements itself primarily through that allegiance, that is too universal to be bribed, too impalpable to be forced, too effective to be ignored.[2]

The notion of cosmopolis is not unrelated to the multifaceted tradition of natural law,[3] with its emphasis on the common good, but it lacks specific concern for the integrity of terrestrial life. All such notions—natural law, the common good, and cosmopolis—await an application to the ecological concerns of our day. There is no question of calling for some kind of police force to implement the ecological concerns that have arisen. That would be self-defeating, and be far from the living communion that Pope Francis and so many others have envisaged. Nevertheless, what has become necessary is genuine communication of the best intelligence and enlightened practice, able to resist the general bias of short-term goals and vested interests.

INTEGRAL ECOLOGY?

Integral ecology begs for closer description. The connotations of the term are largely negative: integral ecology is not realized by ideologically excluding any domain or dimension of knowledge from consideration. Consequently, it envisages, however imperfectly, not only particular ecological niches, or even larger habitats, but the whole terrestrial biosphere: in short, the incomprehensible totality of existence in life (*LS*, esp. chap. 4), to be received as a gift of "a sublime communion" (*LS* 89). This implies the presence of the giver, and the contemplation of what Christians hold to be the apex of divine giving, the incarnation of Jesus Christ: "God so loved the world that he gave his only Son" (John 3:16). All these considerations must figure in any responsible presentation of what is involved in an integral ecology. It may be that some are content with the miserable reduction of the "sublime communion of life" to what is immediately and empirically controllable; or, at the other extreme, they may become so entranced with mystical considerations focusing on life in its ultimate form that they cease to be attentive to what good science is telling us in the present.

Clearly, integral ecology does not begin from a ready-made synthesis of scientific observations. It is always in the making, as it were, in our experience of human bodily consciousness, out of which all scientific specialties emerge, not to replace our immediate experience but to serve it.[4]

In these few remarks, I refer to what is in effect an ecological growth of consciousness characteristic of the present time. Specifically, it suggests that an integral ecology can learn much from a phenomenology disclosing what is going on "at the heart of reason." Rather than take for granted the post-Enlightenment fragmentation of knowledge and the endless proliferation of specializations pointing away from the concreteness of our experience, it is better to immerse oneself in reality as it is given before any rational analysis can occur. There is an embodied experience given in a way that precedes the concept or system or even verbal formula, and any science constructed as an exploration of any specific aspect of reality. Phenomenological attentiveness at "the heart of reason" presupposes that we exist and coexist in the consciousness of

3

being immersed and participating in the inexpressible totality of the universe as it is *given*. In this respect, we fail in not recognizing our embodied participation in the universe as a precondition for all scientific and practical knowledge. It is to foreclose on the range and depth of a genuinely integral ecology.

In the enormity and variety of its achievements, the very success of the Enlightenment eventually worked against the true integration of human knowledge and respect for the totality of experience. Complex cultural and social conditions tended to mute the disclosive power of religious and even philosophical language in the deepest registers of meaning, so that a genuinely integral ecology became impossible. Now, amid this ecological crisis, there is a sad fragmentation of disciplines and a jumble of attitudes and perspectives. The situation deteriorates with conflicts occasioned by mutual rivalry and the diminishing sense of synthesis and communication in a world of competing points of view. As noted in chapter 4, a religious sense of creation provides a background by which all our diverse human creativities can improvise their variations as part of the symphony of reality.

The scientist and philosopher Michael Polanyi, by pointing to the manifold and dynamic structure of human knowing, suggests possibilities of generous collaboration between science, philosophy, ecology, and theology—even if it remains a remote ideal. However, the dynamics of knowing suggest "a continuous ascent from our less personal knowing of inanimate matter to our convivial knowing of living beings and beyond this to the knowing of our responsible fellow men. Such I believe is the true transition from the sciences to the humanities and also from our knowing the laws of nature to our knowing the person of God."[5]

Different degrees or levels of personal knowing help frame questions as to the creativity that has sustained and moved forward the evolutionary self-transcendence of the universe. What is the light of our understanding, and the light in which we participate? What is the primordial unity in which this given totality is a "uni-verse," a coexistence, even a communion, that has enabled the chaos of atoms and molecules, of life-forms and consciousness, of relationships and processes, to emerge as we contemplate it, in awe and responsibility, in this present moment?[6]

Given our concerns for the development of an integral ecology, we find a remarkable instance of both content and collaboration in Bruno Latour's *Inquiry into Modes of Existence: Anthropology for Moderns.*[7] It provides a valuable resource for the integral ecology we are envisaging. In fact, this whole project appears to have its origin in enabling communication between economics and ecology.[8] In presenting his project, Latour contests the flat univocal conception of science in favor of intercommunication between many "modes of existence," and the communities and institutions they represent. He provides not only examples of the content arising out of intercommunication in this way but also gives an example of the networks that can be formed and activated in the interest of a more holistic understanding of human existence and the communication that is necessary. Certainly, our present concern for an integral ecology can profit from this a new anthropology in the making, even if fundamental theological, philosophical, and spiritual dimensions of a genuinely integral ecology are as yet lacking—perhaps because such components may well appear too "religious" for Latour's largely secular interdisciplinary modern anthropology.

Decades ago, I tried to conceive of theology in its content and methods in the light of a growing ecological and even cosmological awareness.[9] It is encouraging to note that such an awareness has entered more strongly into Christian consciousness and even into papal teaching. Here, I explore more thoroughly what I had presented in previous books and articles to bring out more clearly the background, theological and spiritual, against which an integral ecology might take shape. The aim is to evoke a horizon in which a new sense of conscious connection with the biosphere of this earth, with the encompassing cosmic reality and with the singularity of Christian revelation, might come to expression. Certainly, many Christians have an increasing familiarity with the brilliance of the scientific explorations that are taking place, all the way from quarks to quasars, from the Hubble photos to the TV presentations of Sir David Attenborough. This new sense of the mystery of the cosmos is often accompanied by a stirring of ecological conscience in wonder as the universe has brought forth life in all its precious variety. With such an expansion of consciousness in science and moral concern, faith can be temporarily tongue-tied. How can our Christian vision encompass the wonder and responsibility that a new sense of reality inspires? How can faith make these new connections?

There is no universal standpoint outside the entire process: you can only enter the conversation with what you are and the cultural resources you bring. For my part, essential aspects of what I am and where I come from are Christian faith, the Catholic tradition, and the disciplines of theological exploration and philosophical reflection. More immediately, my viewpoint is affected by the degree to which I have let that faith, that tradition, and those disciplines be sparked into a new intensity of exploration by new holistic, ecological, and cosmic perceptions of reality. Unless we are to be progressively schizophrenic, somehow, we need to make sense of it all.

HUMILITY OF THE AMATEUR

It requires no special modesty to admit that we do not know everything about everything. Neither do I think it is an excess of humility to disclaim knowing even something about everything. Still, while writing, I often returned to one of the most enduring philosophical insights, from Aristotle to Teilhard—namely, that in each of us is something about everything, or at least, somebody in the everything, or even everything in the somebody we each are: the microcosm within the macrocosm, the image of God within the universe of God's creation. To bring that to consciousness—to cultivate this "en-globing" sense of belonging to the whole, to throw light on our existence as an overture and coexistence within the all, to intimate the horizon in which we can understand our participation in the emergence of the universe—strikes me as a worthwhile goal.

Yet there is a risk in attempting such a thing. You have to work in terms of intimation and evocation. It is like suggesting a feel for creation as a poem before you read it as a work of prose. To specialists, such efforts sound irritatingly vague. General statements are often the resort of very limited competence in dealing with so many areas. However, in this remarkable age of specialization, we are not used to thinking in the largest possible terms.

Nevertheless, I am disposed to defend an amateur status in this new age of ecological connections. To suggest that we are all amateurs when it comes to "getting it all together" implies no arrogant judgment on the expertise and intelligence of others—be it in science, theology, or philosophy—who have been exploring different dimensions of these cosmic and global matters. The universe, as it emerges into our present apprehensions, does not, in fact, encourage professionals and specialists. In some ways, it favors the amateur. And this is in two senses of the word. First, in that we are all beginners in the presence of the overwhelming complexity of things. Though some might have a remarkable competence in one or other or even several of the relevant disciplines, there is simply no room for the cosmic know-all. Challenged to a universal vision, none of us can be so full of ourselves as to render further discussion useless. Things are too big for that, and, on the shadow side, too far gone, if we dare face either the ecological destruction that has occurred in the world, or the distress occurring in the inner ecology of our various cultures.

But there is a second sense of *amateur*, an older and more tender one. In its Latin roots, it means quite simply, "lover," one who does things for the joy of cherishing something deemed to be of essential value. This is a meaning I especially treasure in the present context. It captures a sense of not waiting for the grand solution, but of starting from where we are and making the best of it, by throwing our best selves into the whole business. If you left love or art or communication to the professionals, we would hardly begin to live.

Furthermore, in the deep reaches of faith, there is value in maintaining an amateur status. There are no professionals in the sight of God; we are saved neither by the knowledge or the good works of someone else. For we enter the kingdom as amateurs, as lovers, as children, and as eternal beginners. This is especially the case, perhaps, when it comes to making new connections with the wonder of life and the universe itself.

In this regard, an integral ecology includes an ecology of meaning, with the accent on connections, interconnections, implications, and analogical linkages—a version of that "framework for collaborative creativity" commended by Bernard Lonergan.[10] However, "framework" is perhaps too much a metaphor of stability, given the spiraling pattern of interweaving connections that are possible. Hopefully, such an exploration will lead to a deeper, broader understanding of what "catholic" (*kat' holou*, "in accord with the whole") might mean today.

With this ecological catholicity, Christian thinking expands to meet the demands of the age, and comes into its own as a great intellectual adventure. As faith works to express its meaning in the light of new modes of understanding the universe and in the context of a new ecological awareness of our planetary coexistence, there are many ways to proceed. Yet, now, we are still at the point of inklings, anticipations, and partial viewpoints regarding what might emerge.

As faith slowly familiarizes itself with the methods and achievements of current explorations of life on earth within this universe, we begin to learn a new language of integral ecology, more worthy of the limitless mystery within which we exist. For too long, the language of faith has been a local dialect. But this now has a chance to grow into a genuinely universal communication and gracious wholeness. For its part, the light of faith has begun to play on the whole mystery of life and to illuminate the universal scope of knowledge, of what is, and what might emerge.

Christian faith must always be looking for a method adequate to articulate the meaning of its reality and significance of its vision. In today's ecological optic within an expanding cosmological horizon, theology is being reinvigorated with the excitement of learning. This has already happened in terms of the fundamental documents or doctrines of faith: enormous progress has been made in biblical and historical studies. But there remains "the book of nature" to be read as a kind of primary revelation accessible to all. Theology has already achieved a new comprehension of social reality in the variety of liberation and political theologies. But such modes of reflection eventually give rise to deeper questions concerning planetary coexistence with all living things. Furthermore, the increasing dialogue with other religious traditions and worldviews suggests what we all have in common. Yet neither our differences nor our agreements can let us forget our common earthly origins and responsibilities.

THEOLOGY AND ECOLOGY

The explorations of theology move on through a critical scrutiny of the primary biblical and doctrinal data, to a compassionate social praxis, and in dialogue with all peoples of wisdom and good will. Yet this must be set within the unfolding of a longer, larger, all-inclusive story of creation and its relation to the emergence of the universe itself and the evolution of life on this planet. When the gospel story is told within such a narrative, faith begins to reach to its deepest roots in the earth, and to stretch out into hitherto unimaginable dimensions of the cosmos.[11]

In this new context, faith, working through hope and love, continues "to seek understanding," *fides quaerens intellectum*, as the time-honored Anselmian phrase has it. Three traditional techniques continue to be helpful and will have later applications in this work as we go.

First, the way of analogy. By using models, metaphors, and symbols drawn from experience, we move from the known to the unknown, to arrive at a partial but more integrally ecological sense of the whole, whether we treat of life on earth, the distinctiveness of human creation, the trinitarian source and end of all that is, or the life of the world to come and creation transformed.

Second, by way of interconnection. Systems of meaning are constructed by making connections between different articles or aspects of faith in relation to nature and grace to form an ordered, one might say, holographic, vision of God's self-communication to the world. For example, the mystery of the incarnation can shed light on the meaning of the sacraments; just as the Eucharist, for instance, can suggest ways of understanding how the Spirit is present and active in the world, especially once the incarnation is appreciated as expanding in the resurrection and ascension of Christ.

Third, theology seeks to speak to the dynamics of hope, and to the search for meaning and fulfillment. It must immerse its religious expression in the stream of humanity's common search for the fullness of life, the ultimate in human destiny. The meaning of faith is meant to be liberating, leading to a greater conduct of freedom, yet opening to that future that only God can give.

9

The dramatic and often heroic articulations of liberation theology move in this direction.

In the present scientifically informed culture, such analogies, interconnections, and ultimate reference need to operate in a field incredibly extended in comparison with the past. An expanding universe, an evolutionary world, a relational and holistic understanding of all reality, all demand a theology that can grow with the universe of our perception. Reflective faith, therefore, must work with analogies drawn, for example, from quantum mechanics, evolutionary process, and ecological interaction. The old views of nature, of matter, of substance, even of causality, will not do. The unchanging "great chain of being" that structured the mental space of past thought for millennia must now be interlinked within the processes that have occurred, and are occurring, in time.

Perhaps the deepest change in the style of analogical thinking comes in the realization that the whole universe of reality is one great process of evolutionary emergence. While there are distinctions, hierarchies, and differentiations to be observed in the given plurality of living and nonliving things, all are alike insofar as they are interconnected with the one process of universal becoming. The cosmos, therefore, is to be understood as a vast analogical event.[12] If analogy is knowledge made possible by extrapolating from one frame of reference and connection to another, it is now seen, not so much as an improbable stretching of the imagination from one order of being to another, but as the only way of approximating to the concrete, dynamic unity-in-difference that the actual universe represents.

As there are new resources for analogical thinking, so too there are new interconnections to be made. The connections that faith might make among its own specific truths need now to be related to the world of interconnections and communication that science has discovered.

If new analogies recommend themselves, and if there are new connections to be made, there is also a new form of universal hope to be expressed. Faith must learn to speak of human destiny not simply out of a laudable concern to save our souls, but in terms of the emergence and destiny of the universe. Theology is faced with its most important question: how daring and inclusive might our hope be?

In all this, reflective faith has much to learn, and in that learning, to contribute what is unique to it. The light of faith is shining in a radiant universe literally aglow with cosmic radiation in evidence of its explosive beginnings. NASA's Cosmic Background Explorer (COBE) satellite is enabling scientists to backtrack nearly fourteen billion years to the first three hundred thousand years of our cosmic beginnings. The photos taken by the Hubble telescope are an inexhaustible source of wonder at the beauty and the extent of the universe in which we exist. In that world of stupefying dimensions of time and space, the light of faith is another kind of "background radiation," inviting the human mind not to miss the whole point of existence, and the wonder of the universe itself. The "faith seeking understanding" of theological tradition finds new expression by participating in an integral ecology.

In other words, theology and philosophy, in their ongoing search for wisdom, have begun to respond to all the colors of the spectrum. We no longer live in the old simplicities of black and white. For we find ourselves in an astonishingly vast, subtle, and beautifully differentiated universe of many colors. With this new sensitivity to the variegated radiations of the light, faith can adore the One who dwells in the radiance of "unapproachable light" (1 Tim 6:16).

Metaphors aside, a new sense of interconnection leading to a new comprehension of the whole is taking place. Most importantly, it is a new savoring of the mystery of life in its origin, its end, and in all its present manifestations. Faith has its own intimacy with the meaning of life and the gift of our existence; in the words of the psalm, all living beings

> feast on the abundance of your house,
>   and you give them drink from the river of your
>   delights.
> For with you is the fountain of life;
>   in your light we see light.
>
> (Ps 36:8–9)

For instance, as we begin to comprehend the destruction that has occurred in the tiny span of recent human history, the negativities of the situation can be appalling. Add to this the tides of information that wash over our minds from the dozens of relevant sciences and the hundreds of activist groups, and we soon find that our minds are overloaded.

Obviously, there is a marvelous heightening and expansion of consciousness in integral ecology, along with an awareness of the ambiguous and even destructive relationship of the human with the millions of species of living things within the commonwealth of life on earth. While this can intensify awareness of the beauty, the fragility, the sheer chanciness of our existence, there is a special strain as well. To touch on such limits is to be driven back to the most sustaining sense of reality. Twenty-three centuries ago, Aristotle averred that the human spirit was in some way all things.[13] But it is no easy matter, psychologically speaking, to be open to the universe, especially as contemporary sciences are revealing it. The new vision not only disorients the mind, as any number of the pioneers of quantum physics confessed;[14] it also disturbs the conscience as new values, new cares, new responsibilities make their presence felt. Given the complexity of the situation, any inherited synthesis of meanings and values suffers a crisis. The century past has known enough of the destructive force of totalitarian ideologies such as Marxism and National Socialism and even today's consumerist capitalism. The current enthusiasm for ecology may possibly give rise to its own range of ideologies, as Murray Bookchin, a noted ecologist, warns:

> Vital as "interconnectedness" may be, it has often been the basis of beliefs…that become the means for social control and political manipulation. The first half of the twentieth century is in great part the story of brutal movements like National Socialism that fed on a popular anti-rationalism, anti-intellectualism and a personal sense of alienation. They mobilised and homogenised millions into an anti-social form of perverted "ecologism" based on intuition, "earth, blood and folk," indeed and "interconnectedness"…[and] eventually turned much of Europe into a huge cemetery.[15]

THE ROLE OF FAITH

A rigid ideology is the death of hope and imagination, but here, a reflective faith will have a critical role in the formation of an integral ecology. Referring to faith, Lonergan writes that it is a consciousness born of religious love, that is, a self-transcending consciousness, "brought to a fulfilment, as having undergone a conversion, as possessing a basis that may be broadened and deepened and heightened and enriched but not superseded."[16]

Such faith cannot be superseded. It is a radical, intimate, universal yes in a way that cannot be replaced by a no. Certainly, it can be "broadened and deepened and heightened and enriched"—as it expands into the meanings and values necessary for an integral ecology.

In this regard, faith has both a deconstructive and a constructive role. By resisting any kind of ideological system due to its God-centered vision, Christian experience must nevertheless expand to new dimensions. An ultimate faith, hope, and love are not irrelevant to the formation of an integral ecology. Far from denying the positive attainments of the new sciences, a Christian vision can place all exploration in a context of reconciliation, communion, and, most importantly, hope. Even if the light of faith is experienced as no more than a kind of "background radiation" in many lives of research, art, and social commitment, it still communicates its sense of the universe as a whole, a gift, and an astonishing wonder.

For its part, the Christian vision has a range of resources to offer: theological, moral, spiritual, and philosophical. Add to these the intercultural experiences of its apostolic and patristic beginnings, its medieval synthesis, and its contemporary commitment, and it becomes a major resource, current thought, and ecological commitment.[17] Faith communicates a sense of creation precisely as a whole. Furthermore, in terms of the genesis of this cosmos, theology sees creation as God's preparation for what has taken place in the incarnation. Consequently, Christians find themselves involved in the earth-centered conversations now taking place. Religious resources for the ecological sphere have entered a more productive dialogical phase, in contrast to the earlier recriminations.[18]

13

In this respect, two areas of possible dialogue are clear: first, the sense of the immense, laboring fertility of the past that has brought us forth and placed us together in this present moment. Second, a growing sense of responsibility for the future that, in some quite new way, will be the product and outcome of present decisions. A "common era" has been forced upon us by the sheer extent of the concerns we must now share. The imperative for each of us and for the great classic traditions that have nourished the human enterprise is to throw our best selves into the mix. No one has cornered all the good energies of faith and love, of justice, tenderness, and wisdom. And, no matter how we look at the situation, this imperative is still needed for creative spiritual energies to inspire hope for the future.

A fundamental sense of community is the first requirement of any effective ecological commitment. But it is precisely on this level of community that increasing alienation has been most obvious. The abstraction and disaffection of the human from nature, and the violence and antagonism of human beings among themselves, have long been the cause of alarm. Huge alliances have been formed along political, economic, racial, sexual, cultural, and religious lines. Political, economic, and social superstructures have evolved to serve an alienating situation so that the common good is at best understood as a compromise among competing groups of self-interest and greed. In such a context, ecology can easily restrict its aims to environmentalism and merely landscaping areas of poisoned earth.

CHURCH AND ECOLOGY

There is no straightforward way simply to legislate the structures necessary to maintain the quality of the biosphere. Even if such structures might conceivably be legally enforced in an ecological cosmopolis, the deep values and meanings necessary in a critical situation cannot be decreed into being. Legislative bodies can change laws, but they cannot change hearts. That can only come about by an inspired sense of community and solidarity. It is on this level, that of the deep structures of human belonging and shared hope, that the Church can redefine its role.

The Christian churches, with their resources of moral traditions and religious vision, must seize the opportunity to offer a unique service at this historical moment. However, this community-forming ministry of the Church can only operate within larger pursuits of planetary community. Though it is an international institution, with its own long history in the development of Western civilization, the Church is not a world to itself. In times past, it has been the carrier of intellectual and moral values that have deeply affected culture and human civilization. But now the worlds of intelligence and moral values have expanded so much that the Church must reshape itself as both a teacher and a learner in this new situation. The novelty of the situation is most evident in the world of science, but also regarding the morality of human rights and the further extension of this into the area of interfaith dialogue—in an ecological context.

As it works within this always-larger world of intelligence, moral-ity, and religion, the Christian Church has both a redemptive and a constructive role. All forms of community are vulnerable to the baleful influence of the seven deadly sins: pride and greed, envy and apathy, violence and dishonesty remain ever apt to frustrate the possibilities of collaboration in the common good. By witness-ing to its conviction that forgiveness and reconciliation are real possibilities for human existence, no matter how godforsaken the historical situation seems to be, no matter what the extent of the failure and destructiveness present in any past, the Church acts within culture to assist in diagnosing the general plight. In its wit-ness to limitless mercy, the Christian community encourages the integrity required to confess our social sins for what they are, and to renew hope even when healing seems impossible. Without such honesty and hope, any culture is locked in an endless rationalizing regarding its deepest failures. When sins are confessed in the hope of forgiveness and reconciliation, a new beginning can be made. Hope enables us to imagine the world otherwise. For our history is not the sum of our failures. The last word, at least in any Christian statement, is one of grace and limitless mercy.

More positively, the Church has a constructive role in the global and ecological turn in human consciousness. Christian faith lives in a familiarity with the universe as the one creation of God. It surrenders in adoration to that mystery of Love that created the world to communicate itself completely to what is other than itself. Such love is the field of life-giving, transforming energy pervading all creation. In those who surrender to it, the energy of God's Spirit inspires a totality, a uni-verse, of all things in Christ, along with an outreach to what is most forgotten, vulnerable—the suffering neighbor in whatever form she or he or it is present. Distinctively, such faith celebrates its sense of the divine presence within creation in the sacramental forms of its worship. There, the humble realities of our world become icons of the mystery at work. From beginning to end, and in each conscious moment, the Christian universe is one of ever-original gift, of self-giving relationality, and of ongoing transformation. If "ecology" in its Greek roots signifies "the meaning of the home," Christian faith can find a new homecoming through ecological awareness and concern.

As faith seeks new connectedness with the earth, it promotes conversion to a more authentic standard: the currency of inner capitalism has to be exchanged for real values. The realization that "we are up to our necks in debt" to the world of nature[19] tempts us to file for bankruptcy, or to leave the country before the debtors find us. But where can we hide? Hence the pressing need for an integral ecology as we are explaining it.

Just as despair is fundamentally a failure of imagination, real hope is formed out of the active imagination of those who have the humility to recognize this earth as the shared body of our existence. Imagination regains its courage when it is prepared to diagnose the harm caused by the refusal of our earthly status. More positively, creativity is newly inspired to the degree we give ourselves to a more intimate collaboration with the gracious mystery of Life, however it has been revealed to us.

In ecological terms, we are being invited into an embodied awareness in the interconnected, multiform life of the planet itself. The human person is newly perceived as an "earthling" in the great temporal and spatial genesis of the cosmos itself. In other words, a new sense of self is being born, characterized by a humility that accepts dependence on a world of living and nonliving things for its existence, nourishment, and delight. The great Barbara Ward, writing decades ago, captured a basic point:

When we confront the ethical and natural context of our daily living, are we not brought back to what is absolutely basic in our religious faith? On the one hand, we are faced with the stewardship of this beautiful, subtle, incredibly delicate, fragile planet. On the other, we confront the destiny of our fellow man, our brothers. How can we say that we are followers of Christ if this dual responsibility does not seem to us the essence and heart of our religion?[20]

Christians have to repent of their sins; and it might be no small service to give the lead here. Each one of the seven deadly sins has an anti-ecological connotation: pride—the rejection of the humility of the human scale; covetousness—defining oneself in terms of having, rather than being; lust—the denial of the sacredness of life and relationship; anger—the extreme intolerance that sees all diversity as a threat; gluttony—the destructive consumption of precious common resources; envy—self-absorption that permits no gratitude or joy in the diversity of gifts; and sloth—expecting nature and life to give us a free ride! There can be no real collaboration without acknowledging failure and powerlessness, and asking forgiveness for falling short of the great commandments of love, and for failing to live out the whole logic of the incarnation of God among us. Still, Christian life, in the essential energies of its faith, hope, and love, has more to offer than the seven deadly sins of Christian failures. Grace keeps on being grace, and the healing and hope it offers can be a beneficent influence in the great concerns of the moment.

ROOTS AND CONNECTIONS

The scope of a repentant and reconciling Christian holism can be helpfully traced in the roots of three key words: *ecology, religion,* and *catholicity*.

First, *ecology*: this word has been in use little more than a century after being coined by the German zoologist Ernst Häckel. Its Greek roots imply "the meaning of the home," as has been mentioned. Consequently, it came to refer to the study of the complex totality of conditions necessary for the survival of specific living organisms. By stressing the complexity of relationships characteristic of a given organism, it not only emphasizes the importance of such coexistence, but also raises the question of the extent to which living things are fundamentally *living relationships*. The exploration of such interconnectedness reveals how living things, whatever their species, are truly at home in earth. As a new science of wholeness, ecology explores the "home," the *oikos*, as the matrix of all the relationships of living beings, where each living thing is at home and has a livelihood. Thus, ecology explores nature "in the round," so to speak, in all the intricate, delicate interactions that characterize life on this planet. Terrestrial life is, therefore, a community of communities in which no species is just an isolated specimen living by and for itself, but a participant in a living, interconnected totality.[21]

The second key word is *religion*. The Latin roots are instructive: *religare* (to bind together again) or *re-eligere* (to renew one's choice). A fresh comprehensiveness of faith and action is implied. The religion of this time must aim to tie our experience together in greater wholeness, and to choose the path of wholeness for shared healing and common health. A deeper, more tender bonding to the earth and the wonder of life will help us see life, not as a bundle of problems to be solved, but primarily as a gift, a shared connectedness within a life-giving mystery. The problem in recent centuries has been that our religious sense has not notably linked us back to the earth, nor into the whole communion of living things.[22] The result is an odd attenuation of Christian experience. For, with its accent on creation, the incarnation of the Word, the resurrection of the body, and the sacramental character of the divine presence, Christian faith is, in so many ways, the most earthy and material of all religions.

Our third word is *catholic*, from the Greek *kat' holou*, literally, "universal," "all-embracing," "in accord with the whole." It has, of course, its original historical meaning in the self-description of the Catholic Church, in its institutional intent to welcome the whole—the totality of God's revelation and the totality of Christian response in all the variety of cultures and languages in which they occur. But whatever our specific Christian traditions—Catholic, Orthodox, Anglican, Protestant—catholicity is generally

accepted as a mark of the authenticity of faith. It remains, therefore, a mark of fundamental Christian concern; but now it awaits a
larger application in an ecological and cosmic frame of reference.
Such catholicity evokes a more expansive way of indwelling creation as participants in the totality of the mystery revealed there,
in the one mystery of Christ, "and in him all things hold together"
(Col 1:17). Here Simone Weil's question is pertinent: "How can
Christianity call itself Catholic if the universe is left out?"[23]

This cursory reference to the classical derivations of these key
words suggests a far more serious search for roots. How might
the sense of the living planetary whole extend the wholeness that
Catholic faith pretends to celebrate? How is the whole marvelous
web of life on this planet to be integrated into the Catholic sense
of "grace healing, perfecting, and elevating nature," in a way that
makes connections with the Catholic doctrines of Creation, Trinity, incarnation, sacrament, and natural law? How, in short, in
the face of the eco-catastrophe that threatens planet Earth today,
might a Catholic sense of the universe welcome and promote a
more profound ecological commitment?

CONCLUSION

One can hardly doubt that some enormous change is called for
in human culture, in our individual lifestyles, in the expression
and practice of our faith. There is an anxiety inherent in the ecologically critical turning point we have been considering.[24] Will it
really become a turnabout, a conversion of the religious, moral,
intellectual, and spiritual dimensions that is necessary?

The concluding lines of E. F. Schumacher's *Guide for the Perplexed*
offer salutary advice:

> Can we rely on it that a "turning around" will be accom-
> plished by enough people quickly enough to save the
> modern world? This question is often asked, but no
> matter what the answer, it will mislead. The answer
> "Yes" would lead to complacency, the answer "No" to
> despair. It is desirable to leave these perplexities behind
> and to get down to work.[25]

In that spirit, we will continue with this search for connections, as a tiny ingredient in the large conversation on the meaning of life and of our place in it. Each of us has to enter the conversation from where we are, owning that standpoint with humility and hope, for we are not alone in the universe, and with compassion. We are all involved together in the great drama of life, stirring to the intimations of a new vision and a more genuinely ecological conversation. It is a matter of understanding our lives as an ever-expanding, open circle of living communion.

CHAPTER 2

Contexts

A N INTEGRAL ECOLOGY must respect several contexts if it is to be genuinely dialogical and inclusive; it extends beyond the boundaries of the science of ecology. The ecological cannot be separated from the social and the cultural, just as these cannot be abstracted from a philosophical and religious view of the world. Furthermore, a true ecological approach must integrate questions of justice in debates on the environment to hear both "the cry of the earth and the cry of the poor" (*LS* 49). There are always larger contexts. In this chapter, we select three contextual considerations, the better to face the questions that arise, and suggest the contribution integral ecology might make:

1. The Larger Story
2. A New Paradigm?
3. A New Age?

THE LARGER STORY

When exploring the possibility of an integral ecology there is a problem: The very plurality of sciences results in very different perspectives and, as a result, more refined specializations. Consequently, it is difficult to have a meeting of minds, let alone an integration of concerns regarding the deeper issues that affect our humanity. Some degree of polarization is inevitable, and efforts to defend one's territory at all costs are not unknown. Many conflicts have their origin in the lack of a shared story regarding the origins of the universe and the history of life on this planet. However, the very fact that we are earthlings existing and even coexisting within this particular universe surely suggests that we have something in common, and that collaboration for the well-being of the planet has become urgently desirable, even if different points of view are inevitable. Regarding collaboration, specializations and the possibility of conflict arise from the complementary nature of human exploration, since no one avenue is adequate. Conflicting attitudes may also arise from various stages in the history of possible collaborations. The accumulated wisdom of astronomers and even astrologers gazing at the night sky over millennia is not the same as having access to the photographs taken by the Hubble telescope. Conflicts, of course, can be far more deep-seated than different perspectives or various stages of history, as when a specific domain of science might rule that deeper philosophical or theological questions are beyond the pale, and have no place in an integral ecology.

In view of such conflicts, there is value in continuing to explore some version of a common story of origins as it includes the explorations of the present, however implicitly that might be. To the degree we find something in common, say in the story of life on this planet, the clash of different points of view will be less discordant. Here cosmologists recall that the universe has resulted from an event that occurred some 14.8 billion years ago, and that the cosmos is still expanding, so that light from far distant objects has farther to travel in order to reach us in our planetary home. Here, too, we must stress that important events are always unfolding; the only way to come to any understanding of them is to participate in that unfolding—so to get a feel for what an integral ecology will demand.

Creation as Event

For this reason, it is worth pausing on the origin of the universe as an event. In its all-englobing and expanding impact, the emerging universe is not circumscribed by any concept of reality or anticipation. It is always inexpressible in its scope and implications, and outside any calculus of cause and effect. The origins and effect of this primordial event can never be fully grasped, despite their expanding impact. In its "excess," this primordial event disrupts any prior metaphysical theory or comprehensive explanation. Historically, for instance, the tragic event of the First World War is still largely inexplicable in destructiveness. It overflowed the bounds of any settled horizon of rationality. More positively, the historical emergence of Christianity and, indeed, other world religions are events of world-shaping proportions. Attempts to reduce such events to circumscribable objects serve only to blind rationality to the overwhelming character of what has taken place.

The French philosopher Claude Romano helpfully distinguishes a mere event from a far more significant happening. A mundane, factually recorded event is impersonal in its objectivity. It has no existential import. It is datable as a *fait accompli*—an innerworldly empirical fact. In contrast, there is an event of another kind. This happens beyond all previous calculations and intimately involves those caught up in it. Its impact leads to world-changing decisions, for the world of one's previous life is reconfigured, and made newly meaningful and significant, outside the logic of cause and effect. Events in this sense give rise to a certain "anarchy," as the fixed points of previous horizons are dramatically shifted. Consequently, the full significance of the event in question can only emerge with time, as it awaits a future to unfold.[1] The self is caught up in an incalculable existential venture, not as a passive recipient, but as an active participant. In this respect, it is not a matter of projecting new possibilities on an already established world, but of living in a new register of existence—within a world newly understood. Something has occurred from outside any previous individual horizon. A convenient example, again, is one's own birth—or that of others. For each birth is an event that occurs as given from beyond, yet at the same time it opens possibilities that are not predetermined against any settled horizon.[2] And, of course, in the largest possible domain, the emergence of the universe and the origin of life on this planet is at once a gift and the limitless scope of mystery. To accommodate Romano's usage, everyone and everything is an *advenant*, in the sense of being caught up and carried forward in the adventure of life, in an incalculable solidarity and interaction with all other living things on this planet, and as a participant in the existence of the universe itself.

Philosophers usually speak about historic events of such magnitude affecting the world so that it can never be the same again. Essentially, we, and all life, are the outcome of an original event that gave rise to the formation of this planet and life on it, with its 4.5 billion years of evolutionary development. While a patient scientific reconstruction of what happened so many billion years ago offers a precious perspective, it would be naïve to think that such a narrative reconstruction explains all life, all culture, all hope, and all intelligence, and thereby presents a universal theory or story of everything.

This is not to argue that the scientific story of our origins and common belonging is of little human importance.[3] Nevertheless, if this scientific narrative suppresses classic religious narratives of Creation as found in Genesis and the New Testament presentation of everything created in the Word of God and holding together in Christ, careful consideration is necessary lest the whole challenge of an integral ecology be compromised from the beginning.[4]

Let us begin at the more general inclusive point. What is the *significance* of the four-and-half-billion-year story of our planet, of the more than fourteen-billion-year story of the emergence of the cosmos in all its differentiation, growing consciousness, and connectedness? So much time has gone into the making of the present that it must point beyond the disillusionment and disappointment. Surely, such a long unfolding of life is not meant to climax in the frenzied consumerism of present culture or leave us at the brink of self-extinction in an increasingly perilous present. Awareness of the whole groaning totality of the past assures us that life must be more than *this*. How, then, can an inclusive scientific story be narrated in a way that is truly hopeful, even though death is a condition of life and the collapse of the cosmos as we know it is a matter of soberly predictable fact?

It can be told most vividly when the objective statements of science are embodied in the flesh and feeling of imagination. It is imagination that gives body and momentum to the way we view the world, and takes the necessary abstractions of theory into a more full-bodied sense of reality. Objective data neatly recorded on the computer screen is refashioned into a narrative of origins.

Contexts

Take the following illustration: It is generally estimated that the earth is about 4.6 billion years old. To grasp such a length of time, consider a forty-six-year-old mythical human accompanying this entire process, with each year representing one hundred million years.[5] On this timescale, you would have to wait till you are forty-two before you thrill to the sight of a flower and smell the fragrance of a bloom. Then, four months into your present forty-seventh year, you will have the special companionship of the mammals: you will see the whale blowing off the coast; the monkeys swinging in the trees; the great cats stalking through the jungles, as you begin to wonder whether you could ever tame a dog or ride a horse. But then, just four hours before midnight on the last day of your forty-seventh year, another more intimate form of companionship will have been offered you. You respond to the smile of a human face.

In the next three hours leading up to your forty-seventh birthday, after various attempts at conversation, you will have worked out with your human companions how to plant a tree and tend a crop. In that last hour, you will have exchanged many skills in building and trading; in recording and writing; in making art and, more ominously, in making war. But only in this last minute, the whistle of the great factories will be heard and their smoke begins to darken your town, as planes fly overhead, and cars fill the roads. You may notice too that some of the great forests have been cut down and that many of your old companions among the birds and the fish, the flowers and trees exist no more, as you thread your way through the rubbish dumps of the great cities, and hear rumors of wars that could destroy the planet itself.

You are forced to wonder what, of all the beauty and variety of such life, will be there in the morning, to celebrate your forty-seventh birthday. Indeed, speaking of the last two hundred years, Thomas Berry, one of the geological storytellers of our day, makes an incisive remark:

> During this period, the human mind lived in the narrowest bonds it has ever experienced. The vast mythic, visionary, symbolic world with its all-pervasive numinous qualities was lost. Because of this loss, humanity made its terrifying assault upon the earth with an

25

irrationality that is stunning in enormity while we were being assured that this was the way to a better, more humane, more reasonable world.[6]

Given the onset of this Anthropocene era, the designation *Homo sapiens* comes to signify not so much a fact, but a hope that we human beings will have the wisdom to face the crisis brought about by misdirected energies. Recent centuries have certainly seen periods of remarkable scientific discovery, geographical exploration, and economic innovation and development. Our planet has been gradually drawn into a single system of technical and material interdependence. The global scale of development has inexorably increased the strain upon the planet's resources and upset the delicate biological mechanisms that have sustained life on earth. Human history is being forced to take fresh bearings as to what ongoing life on this planet might entail. In the era of the Anthropocene, there is need for both a new sensibility regarding the wonder and fragility of the biosphere, and of a new sense of solidarity in global destiny of life on planet Earth.

The very fact that we are earthlings existing within this universe surely suggests that, despite all differences, we have something in common, and that collaboration for the well-being of the planet is possible and urgently desirable. Hence, there is the value of continuing to explore some version of a common story of origins.

A NEW PARADIGM

In the Western philosophical and theological tradition, the virtue of wisdom (*sapientia*) is the ability to judge and order reality from the most radical standpoint.[7] It suggests a taste (*sapere* means "to taste") for the deepest realities of life. True wisdom flows from intuitive familiarity with the whole of nature, resulting in what is termed "connaturality."[8] This was understood as a sense of wholeness and depth that exceeded the calculations of human ingenuity and reason. Thus, wisdom suggests a sense of reality born out of a loving familiarity with, and a deep immersion in, the whole mystery of life. This classical notion easily translates into our present need of a fresh sense of the totality of life, and of more profound, relational participation in the wholeness of existence.

Such wisdom is necessary to grasp what an integral ecology entails, along with a sense of the totality of reality and our human position within it. Technological "know-how" must redefine its aims and capacities, just as the arrogance of "know-all" needs to find a new humility before the vastness and complexity of reality in all its relationships and connections. There has never been more need for a truly integral ecology. The development of a holistic view of nature is resisted by the prevailing one-dimensional, fragmented, instrumental relationship of science and technology. Likewise, the spiritual or theological attitude must reach out to all kinds of exploration through dialogue with the relevant ecological sciences—economics, politics, cultural studies, and others.

A truly integral ecology requires what is frequently referred to as "a new paradigm" for the interactions of the various forms of human knowledge in the planetary conversation that is now taking place.[9] Consequently, the word *paradigm* carries a rich variety of meanings, values, associations, and feelings. More generally, it connotes an overall sense of reality and of our participation in it. More negatively, a *new* paradigm is called for when former ways of understanding and conduct no longer work. In other words, the map that we have been using has become too inaccurate, or incomplete or roundabout. To move forward, we seek a new point of entry into the unknown. What is most needed is a provisional sense of what lies ahead, and of the varied possibilities of moving toward it, while being alert to the precise character of the terrain. Early Australian explorers, in their expeditions into the interior of the continent, expected to find an inland sea, but to their embarrassment, they found instead a desert. Something similar occurred when science discovered that space is not filled with ether, and that subatomic realities are not like small billiard balls, just as earlier, scientists eventually had to face the fact that the sun does not circle the earth, and that the world did not begin five and a half thousand years ago.

The disconcerting element in any new vision is the presence of the human mind and heart, the mysterious dimensions of human consciousness itself. This is capable of endless differentiations, as in the rigorous objectivity of the scientist, the creativity of the artist, the unutterable experience of the mystic, and in the everyday patterns of communication and action in the daily life of the whole human world.[10]

All such forms of consciousness can be enriched and expanded. Take the religious domain, for example, when the believer begins to experience the mystery of God more fully and deeply; or the scientific domain, when investigators are confronted by evidence to which they had been previously blind; or in social justice, when conscience might stir new responses in dealing with one's neighbor or the neighborhood in ways that had not previously troubled the routine patterns of social concern.

By promoting awareness of the interactive totality of living things, as in a new paradigm, an integral ecology is preeminently an awareness of relationships, especially of those relationships, either newly discovered or too long ignored, with the earth itself, with the biosphere of this planet, and within the emergent process of the cosmos itself.

An integral ecology represents a disturbing choice. Upsetting the unreflecting self-satisfaction of any one specific view, there is the need for the scientific mentality to be open to religious and philosophical considerations. Here, most of the terms employed—such as self-transcendence, the dynamism of knowledge and intentionality, the events of conversion, the structure and differentiations of consciousness—enjoy a widespread respectability through the writings of Bernard Lonergan, above all, his *Insight* and *Method in Theology*. Understood in this way, integral ecology is inherently open and flexible, and proportionately applicable to all fields of learning.

Some suggest five features of this *integral ecology*.[11] First, there is a shift *from the part to the whole*. In contrast to the atomistic, analytical approaches characteristic of Bacon, Newton, and Descartes, contemporary holistic and ecological sciences prioritize the interrelational whole of any given reality.

Making such connections is not merely a matter of having a closer "look" at reality. It is rather the outcome of a collaborative method connecting various methods of investigation. These derive from the fundamental dynamics of human consciousness—as in the imperatives Lonergan objectifies: "Be attentive!" (empirical consciousness); "Be intelligent!" (intellectual consciousness); "Be reasonable!" (rational consciousness); "Be responsible!" (moral and affective consciousness).[12]

The second feature of an integral ecology is a shift *from structure to process*. In this respect, structures are manifestations of an underlying process of self-organization. To give a theological example, separate structures of revelation as expressed in the doctrines of Creation, Trinity, incarnation, death and resurrection of Christ, the Church, the sacraments, and the eschatology of the life of the world to come, are now treated in a far more dynamically and integrated manner focused in the one activity of the self-communication of God to creation. Consequently, nature is no longer to be considered as a metaphysically fixed entity, but is rather a heuristic or explanatory notion within the larger dynamics of history and evolution, so that God is the Creator and Sustainer, not of a world of fixed natures, but of a world of time and process.

Third, an integral ecology implies a shift from *the rigorously objective to a more intentionally integrated way of knowing*. Reality is not disclosed by having a good look at something already out there now, however refined our optical instruments might be. The knower is involved in the process, and part of the reality, which is in turn enriched by the understanding and imagination of those who explore it. Lonergan's axiom, "genuine objectivity is the fruit of authentic subjectivity," has a profound application. The truth is discovered to the degree that the full capacities of the knower are involved in sensing, imagining, questioning, pondering, responding, and loving. This is especially instructive in the instances of coming to know another human being, and "the sublime communion of life" in which we exist.[13] Such knowledge is far more vital and intimate compared to just having a good look, or listening more attentively, or dispassionately collecting data on the subject. This understanding of knowledge is similar to that of the scientist-philosopher Michael Polanyi.[14]

Fourth, in the scientific version of the new paradigm, there is a shift *from building a structure to forming a network as the basic metaphor for knowledge*. Rather than merely adding to known reality bit by bit, it is more a question of apprehending the whole in its interconnectedness. To treat anything as a bit or part isolated from the world of relationships in which it exists is to overlook its essential features. If Jacques Maritain, a celebrated French philosopher, promoted *distinguer pour unir*, "to distinguish in order to unite,"[15] as the governing principle of reflection, today the emphasis is reversed. We make distinctions within a prior, fundamental wholeness. The unity of the network precedes the distinctions that are made within it.

Here, too, theology must be aware of its own resources. There is emblematic significance in the fact that the fundamental mystery of Christian faith is the Trinity: the absolute is fundamentally relational; the Divine Persons are self-constituted as "subsisting relationships" grounded in the trinitarian "processions." If God is intrinsically relational, it comes as no metaphysical surprise to find that the universe is relational in its every aspect—a network. The significance of this will be developed later, but beyond this all-important doctrinal focus, the development of theological method itself is more like a network, or, as Lonergan would phrase it, method is "a framework of collaborative creativity."

Fifth, an integral ecology shifts *from clear definitions and neat systems to approximate descriptions and judgments of probability*. Science has abandoned its quest for Cartesian certainty to be content with the more tentative, ever-revisable notion of probability. The human search for truth proceeds by way of an evermore refined series of approximations to what probably is the case. It is not a matter of compressing the world into our scientific models, but of designing models of exploration that illumine our participation in the commonwealth of life on earth within the emergent universe.

The radically inexpressible truth of faith is quite compatible with the successive approximations that history allows. In other words, doctrine develops, and the hierarchy of truths is reshaped and reexpressed. This holistic sense of reality finds expression within the meanings and values that inform a given culture, preeminently those pertaining to the common good and the ecological concerns of our day.

Contemporary culture is deeply affected by the scientific myth, so that the only sure way to knowledge is science, or what passes for it. As a result, our world picture is formed, often enough uncritically, by what are taken to be the findings of science. It is difficult to keep in mind that genuine science is an ongoing, approximate procedure. It employs technical expressions and mathematical symbols of extreme sophistication. In comparison, any prose account is like the wildest kind of poetry. Often, we are left in the position of being simple believers in what they, the scientists, *really* know. A consequent mistrust of our firsthand experience of the world, especially in its religious or artistic or moral dimensions, is predictable. Consequently, it is more socially acceptable to believe in the Big Bang theory than in God's creative Word; easier to believe in the more than 14 billion years of cosmic emergence than in God's creative act.

When science, and the human experience out of which it grows, wakens to its current holistic proportions, the need for a new paradigm becomes clear. And yet there is a disconcerting element in any new holistic vision: to repeat, there is the presence of the human self in the process of exploration when the human mind and heart are involved. In other words, the journey outward into reality needs a firmer connection to a journey inward. That entails being attuned to the mysterious dimensions of human conscious-ness itself—a manifold, endlessly differentiated awareness.

This consciousness is refreshed when new levels of conversion occur, in the distinguishable but interrelated domains of religious, intellectual, moral, and affective development. Through such inte-rior events, conscious existence is enriched and expanded. But an integral ecology is more. Because the reality in which we partici-pate is so pluriform, and because capacities are finite, human con-sciousness must become increasingly differentiated so as to focus critically on this or that dimension of our existence. As a result, different mentalities and specialized modes of understanding are born. Here we note the variety of languages—literary, scientific, mystical, and philosophical—employed to serve each specific "real world" we inhabit. For example, the language of the journalist specializes in communication within the world of the daily con-cerns of the population. The language of scientific theory, unham-pered by the responsibilities of communicating with the laity, is designed to serve the objective expression and exploration of mat-ters so removed from the usual experience that years of training are required to make any sense of the symbols, the terms, and the concerns necessary for the scientific project. For its part, psychol-ogy elaborates a language to express reality "from the inside out," as it were, in terms of the consciousness, self-perception, feelings, and ideas that enable human beings to speak, learn, love, or cre-ate in the first place. As a further complication, artists insist on belonging to a world in a distinctive fashion in their concern to refresh our perceptions of the sheer originality and original beauty of what is experienced—before it can be explained, or used, or explained away. Then mystics, if they speak at all, attempt to give some expression to the intimate presence of ultimate mystery that they have tasted and felt as the origin, ground, and goal of the universe itself.

But a developing integral ecology goes further. The data and the methods of every science have been immeasurably extended and enriched. As a result, a genuinely integral ecology contains fresh elements of conversion along religious, aesthetic, intellectual, or moral trajectories of development. It inspires innovative ways of learning, understanding, and collaborating, while revealing new ranges of values and sensibilities relevant to ecological concerns. By promoting an awareness of the inexpressible *all*, and of the interconnectedness involved, an integral ecology is preeminently an awareness of relationships. It especially focuses on those relationships, either newly discovered or too long ignored, as with the earth itself, with the biosphere of this planet, and within the emergent process of the cosmos itself, and indeed the life-giving Creator Spirit.

An integral ecology, therefore, is a new paradigm, and not an arbitrary option. It is a disturbing choice because it upsets uncritical self-satisfaction in any one view. A scientific mentality needs to be open to religious and philosophical considerations—and vice versa.

This seems the feature of the new paradigm most inimical to theological exploration. After all, faith lives from the conviction that the divine is self-revealed, and that a yes to that cannot turn into a no. But even here, matters are not so cut and dried. First, there is the character of analogical knowledge. Even a council of the Church can allow that, though theological understanding can establish certain likenesses and analogies between normally accessible realities and revealed mysteries, we must always remember that the dissimilarity existing between the creature and the Creator is greater than any similarity.[16] Furthermore, in line with what we have already mentioned, the divinely given "data" are always explored in terms of the limitations and opportunities afforded by a particular stage of history. Even if the yes of faith to the divine mystery is unconditioned and without reservation, the understanding of that faith in its bearing in the real world of our experience is always limited by our pilgrim state. Increase comes from the accumulation of experience and insight. Beyond that, there is a deeper, more interior possibility insofar as believers become more religiously converted to the divine mystery in self-surrender. This can often demand an intellectual conversion, as a reflective faith drops former deficient constructs of imagination or systematic meaning for a more critical objectivity. Ideally, this is linked to a moral conversion as well, as newly discovered values inspire greater responsibility and compassion. Then, too, there is the possibility of a more fundamental enrichment of knowledge, as when the one consciousness becomes more differentiated in its capacities, skills, tastes, feelings, categories, and language.

Therefore, the radically inexpressible truth of faith is quite compatible with the successive approximations that history allows. In other words, doctrine develops, and the hierarchy of truths is reshaped and reexpressed to find expression within the meanings and values that inform a given culture. While faith can and must treasure its intimate experience of God-given truth, a defensive rationalism looking for certitude in each instance of intelligent exploration is deeply inimical to real learning. Theology can be content, then, to join with other forms of thought that are less concerned to trumpet forth the certitude of their attainments, and more inclined to accept the humbler role of exploring the meanings with which the universe is illumined.

Though these remarks on the new paradigm of integral ecology are necessarily general, they suggest the possibility among different methods and disciplines of reciprocal enrichment in a collaborative exploration of our multidimensional universe.

The need for the new paradigms of integral ecology is becoming clearer. The elusive element in any new vision is the mysterious dimensions of human consciousness itself.

A NEW AGE?

The New Age movement as it has taken shape in recent decades is a vast, confusing, often contradictory, phenomenon. Though there is no question of offering a synthesis of this movement, a few typical emphases emerge in the representative literature.[17] In the interests of constructive dialogue, we consider, here, nine points regarding New Age thinking.

First, New Age thinking attempts to counteract a wide range of inherited dualisms in the Western intellectual and spiritual tradition, especially as these were further intensified through the Enlightenment. Hence, a new cosmology of wholeness rejects the separations of science and religion, body and spirit, matter and consciousness, thinking and feeling, male and female, transcendence and immanence, objectivity and subjectivity.

The general problem here, despite the welcome stress on holism, is that *dualism* is often too little distinguished from *duality*. The former implies a distinction in which one element is made ideologically subordinate to the other; whereas the latter is simply an expression of the capacity of human intelligence to distinguish various aspects, or principles, or polarities in the concrete instance. Such distinctions have often been remarkable attainments in the history of thought. The classic example is the duality of body and soul in the constitution of the human being. Hylomorphism understands the material and spiritual to be related in such a way as to constitute the integrity of the embodied, animated, unified reality of the concrete human being. Such an Aristotelian and Thomistic position represents a great advance over the *dualistic* Platonic tradition, which demeaned matter and body and exalted the purely spiritual. There is a danger, then, in this aspect of New Age thinking, to sacrifice the constitutional richness of reality to an undifferentiated confusion: "No one knows better the true meaning of distinction than they who have entered into unity" (Tauler).[18]

Second, in contrast to the doctrine of the transcendence of God over creation, and of the infinite ontological distance between the Creator and the creature, New Age thinking celebrates the immanence of the divine within all things as the ground for a universal interconnectedness.

Such an emphasis can signal a healthy recovery of a genuine sense of the divine presence within all reality. However, the danger is that God is either identified with creation, or is considered simply part of a larger whole. In contrast, the great tradition of theological and philosophical thought considered that the reason for God's unimaginable intimacy with creation lies precisely in the divine transcendence: God is the source and end of all being. Divine transcendence is not opposed to immanence, but is the reason for it. Confusion here draws the accusation that New Age thinking is a regression to paganism and pantheism. What may be struggling for expression is an acceptable form of *panentheism*: all things exist "in God," as their source, ground, and goal. In the Thomistic version of this tradition, God is neither the undifferentiated potentiality of prime matter, nor the soul of the created world, nor the universal process itself. Creation proceeds, rather, from the processive life of the Trinity. It is the dynamic matrix in which the universe comes to be. We shall devote a later reflection to this point.

Third, an intense optimism about individual and social transformation characterizes this New Age movement. The new age has finally dawned; human potential is limitless; its dynamics are beckoning and available. Former views on sin and evil, on the necessity of redemption or the summons to conversion, must yield to a world of God's good creation. Original blessings edge out any consideration of original sin.

We can, of course, delight in the fundamental goodness of creation and the primal originality of God's creative love and grace. But this does not mean repressing the tragedy of the human condition. Our last tragic century hardly permits any innocent optimism. Techniques of meditation and heightening of consciousness, exercises in transpersonal awareness, tantric channeling of energies and the like, can be elaborate subterfuges of denial if the deadly reality of the "heart of stone" is not faced. It comes down to distinguishing between mere optimism and the transcendent character of hope. A hope-filled apprehension of the universe is a high religious achievement. It is attained in the teeth of the problem of evil. It manifests itself in a humble but gracious acceptance of the seemingly random, entropic, and humanly incomprehensible complexity of the universal process. The rhetoric of Christian tradition that would speak of the creation and the fall, of nature and of grace, of conversion from evil and conversion to the good, of the reality of human freedom blossoming only through surrender to the divine, of the cross and resurrection, of the Pauline conflict of flesh and spirit, is evidence of a far more nuanced sense of the human condition than a technique-induced New Age consciousness.[19] Regardless, to say this is to point only to oppositions instead of opening up possibilities of deeper learning on both sides of the divide.

Fourth, and less ambiguously, New Age thinking stresses the planetary dimensions of human consciousness and of ecology itself. The particularities of culture and history, often so defensive and divisive, have to yield to the global dimensions of coexistence. National or even international movements still carry the baggage of specific interests and restricted notions of the common good, when a planetary unity is called for.

The main problem, here, is the way "planetization" occurs. If, on the one hand, it takes place as a genuine ecological communication between all the differentiations of consciousness and all the varied, long-term achievements of human culture, such a convergence of experience, thought, and feeling would indeed promise a new global conscientization. On the other hand, if such a planetization becomes something rather less than this, and more like a marketing of spiritual self-help techniques, a new spiritual consumerism, a new imposition of North American or European postmodern pathologies, New Age planetization will be an oppressive element in the ecology of a global culture. Transcultural communication and cosmic interconnectedness must mean something more than a standardized form of enlightenment.

Fifth, New Age thinking is permeated with a sense of evolutionary consciousness. Imagination links everything in a pan-evolutionary movement. Everything and everyone connects in a universal becoming.

It can hardly be denied that the categories of evolution and emergence are inscribed into contemporary intelligence, as it is manifested in science, philosophy, and theology. The dark side to this evolutionary awareness is in the questions it leaves unanswered, above all, in those of an eschatological nature. Is the present and the past devoid of any meaning, save in reference to our present apprehensions of the future? Was all the suffering of the past just raw material for the New Age? Is there no value in the present save in its evolutionary potential? What of the frustration, failure, waste, tragedy, extinction of species, death of individuals, and the incomprehensible randomness of both the past and the future? Does being vulnerable to all that realm of entropy leave human beings with any meaning at all? Finally, does a simple New Age evolutionary optic tend to place its possessors outside the actual evolutionary process? Are they spared being immersed in it, excused from the demands of patience, surrender, historical memory, and of hope against hope? An evolutionary ideology, contrary to evolutionary science, has a strange way of offering both instant success and a kind of infused knowledge on where things are tending.

The sixth point is more negative, in the way that New Age thinking simply rejects the history of the West. It unwearyingly points out the deficiencies of Newtonian science and Cartesian anthropology. Such an inheritance, it is alleged, narrowed the whole scope of human experience, and diminished the range of alternative modes of perception. The human subject, in the full panoply of consciousness, has been notoriously excluded. This results in a general disaffection with "institutional religion" and with Christianity as its primary instance. The more institutionalized religion became, the more doctrinal its formulations, the more it walled up the sacred in its own mediations, it rendered religious experience inaccessible to its people. With its doctrine of sin and the need for redemption, it demeaned the body and creation, and minimized human potential. Its postmortem promises further alienated its adherents from the material cosmos. A transcendent God from beyond the world offered a precarious salvation to spiritual souls imprisoned within it.

Such a description is not entirely a caricature. And I, along with the generality of theologians and philosophers today, cannot but endorse a return to the subject, if it leads to the reappropriation of the whole scope of human experience. However, matters are more intricate than a leap from one mode of knowing to another without questioning why such agility is justified or possible. Newton's fervent religiosity is well known; but that of Descartes is perhaps more astonishing to the modern holistic mind. It gives us pause to recall that this superrationalist, superindividualist, mathematical French philosopher considered that his discoveries were the result of a visionary experience inspired by Our Lady. Out of such a conviction, he vowed to make a pilgrimage of gratitude to Loreto, which he in fact performed in 1622.[20] Apparently, Descartes was more complex than Cartesianism. So, we are led to ask, what was really going on then? And, what is going on now? Apart from referring to remarks made earlier on historical developments, differentiations of consciousness, and levels of conversion, we add one simple point.

When we attempt to evaluate the past, the actual richness of experience is largely inaccessible to us now. What we are dealing with, unless we are gifted with extraordinary historical imagination, are very narrow objectifications of what was going on in those days, and in those now dead generations, be they Counter-Reformation Catholics, Newtonian scientists, or Cartesian philosophers. Doubtless, the current holistic mentality has developed a much greater refinement in attending to the data of experience and naming it. Still, the real challenge is not one of simply dismissing the narrowness of past achievements, but of integrating all the accessible data into a comprehensive method that does justice to the complexity and richness of reality. It is not enough to have a new guiding symbol of wholeness, nor a more inclusive feeling for the whole, nor even a new scale of values and range of meanings. Some thoroughgoing integration is required, by which we can detect the lacunae or distortions of the past—and of the present, above all, within ourselves. Otherwise, the promise, say, of holistic medicine will be stopped short in its inability to find an answer to the HIV virus; and the desirability of mystical religious experience will be unable to relate to the historical necessity of an institutional form of religion strong enough to confront the enormous social, political, and economic distortions of culture. Why should only oppression and selfishness be institutionalized, and not the forces of self-transcending faith, hope, and love?

In short, a holistic mentality can only be sustained by a holistic method. Otherwise, it will find itself repressing or overlooking whole ranges of data just as effectively as anything in the past.

Seventh, New Age thinking enthusiastically embraces the new physics, the universe of quantum and holographic perception, as more hospitable to the phenomenon of consciousness and transformation. No doubt. Still, we must ask, what is going on in terms of belief? As already noted, our culture is deeply affected by the scientific myth. Consequently, it is easier to believe in the billions of years of cosmic emergence than in the eternal Now that holds all time together; easier to believe in cosmic events taking place in the first trillionth of a second than in providence reaching into every detail of our lives; easier to believe in the hundred billion galaxies extending beyond our Milky Way than in the value of answering the needs of our neighbor; easier to believe in the varieties of quarks than in the value of justice or forgiveness. One can more easily accept refinements of relativity theory—however counterintuitive they appear in the real world of our perception—than the testimonies of prophets or mystics. One can more easily go along with the fundamental four forces unifying the physical universe than with the disclosive power of love; just as one can tend to be more impressed with the authority of the New Physics than any religious or moral tradition, however venerable and ancient. Black holes, or chaos theory, or dark matter are more spontaneously credible than the reality of Christ's resurrection. Popular scientific culture prepares us more for amazement at the genetic connectedness of all life than for the cosmic significance of trinitarian relationships. Cultural belief runs more readily with the incredibly intricate abstractions of the mathematical symbolization of the universe than with the Word who became flesh and dwelt among us.[21]

As already noted, there are many kinds of belief, and in everyday life we are surrounded with proliferating expertise. However, the authenticity of belief is its ability to speak to, or allow for, the whole human condition, always allowing room for the responsible self. Whatever the promise of a holistic mentality or a New Age transformation, each of us must maintain a critical reserve. Any act of belief must send us back to our responsible selves.

The eighth point exhibited by New Age thinking is its "mystical sense" of the universe as a *uni-verse*—a whole, an all—long preceding the specialized analyses and divisions of sciences and the diverse ways of knowing. An anticipation of the whole and an inclusive presentiment of the all have both a long philosophical pedigree. The dynamics of human intelligence are powered by the transcendental notions of the one, the intelligible, the true, the good, the beautiful. Categorically, the mind attains only to the particularity of this or that object within a horizon of the totality of being. Serious contemporary questions arise concerning the nature of this unity. The way Teilhard de Chardin presents the issue documents not only his struggle to formulate a sense of universal event,[22] it also leads us to a distinction of vital importance, if we are to arrive at a genuinely ecological and communal sense of existence. Here is Teilhard's description of two kinds of mystical road:

> The first road: ...to come together with a sort of common stuff which *underlies* the variety of concrete beings. Access to Aldous Huxley's "common ground." This procedure leads ultimately to an *identification* of each and all with the common ground—to an ineffable of de-differentiation and de-personalization. Both by definition and by structure, this is a mysticism WITHOUT LOVE.
>
> The second road: to become one with all...no longer by "dissolution" but through a peak of intensity arrived at by what is most incommunicable in each element. This procedure leads ultimately to an ultra-personalizing, ultra-determining, and ultra-differentiating UNIFICATION of the elements within a *common focus*, the specific effect of LOVE.[23]

Teilhard's "first road" is a conception of a primal, prebiological, and prepersonal unity underlying all things, into which everything ultimately dissolves. Characteristic of his "second road" is the unity based on union with the ultimate, and leading to communion within it. Differentiated realities are not dissolved; they are brought to their interconnected completeness in being. The ultimate unifying force or energy is love, the affirmation of each and all in its irrepeatable particularity. From this love, there flows intimate knowledge of the other; indeed, in Teilhard's understanding—and this accords with the general tradition of Christian theology—such loving knowledge is participation in the creative knowledge and love of God, the source and goal of the universe of particular realities.[24]

The attraction of oriental monistic and mystical philosophies can be easily documented in much New Age thinking. One wonders whether those who follow such a road realize the full import of the choice they have made. At first glance, it would seem to undercut the realism of any ecological commitment, to say nothing of the quality of the transformation of the self that it promises.

At least, the necessity for dialogue is evident: a deeper appropriation of the much-criticized Western tradition (as it appears in Aristotle, Bonaventure, Teilhard, and Lonergan) will, as we will determine, reveal an abundance of overlooked resources.

A mystical resacralization, or reenchantment of nature or science, called for in reaction to the nihilism and mechanicism of recent centuries, will mean something vastly different for those who travel the different roads. For the first, it is a path to dissolution into a formless "all," a unity without difference. For the second, it means participation in a relational universe, an ultimate unity-in-difference.[25]

Finally, New Age thinking relativizes the centrality of the human. Ecologically speaking, the human is one of millions of living species. Cosmologically, the human is a tiny phenomenon occurring within an emergence of cosmic proportions. Anthropocentricity— biblical or otherwise—is, on both counts, a distortion.

We will return to this critical issue; for now, it is significant to note its complexity. Judgments on such a real or possible human self-centeredness remain human judgments. They are made within human consciousness, and are communicated in human speech. Desirably, the relativization of the human indicates an option for humility within the vastness of the cosmos, and for a more profound relationship of care for other species of life that humans have so unthinkingly exploited. Anthropocentricity, a "galloping case of Enlightenment epistemology," needs to be redeemed into a more tender, participative, indwelling kind of knowing.[26] Nonetheless, extreme criticisms of anthropocentricity may mask an effort to escape from the human, to evade the issue of human culture within the ecological commonwealth, and to demean or overlook the role of the human in the unfolding of the cosmos itself. Consequently, then, unwittingly or deliberately, antianthropocentricity is calling for a kind of decapitation of evolutionary process and a suppression of the consciousness in which the wonder of existence emerges.

Admittedly, one who ventures into new perceptions of reality can be criticized as being eclectic. Nonetheless, it is hard to deny the impulse to a deeper search for meaning, a desire to learn by heart the movement and form of the universe in which we so uncannily exist. True, the result is often a strange conglomerate of astrophysics and astrology, of the occult and the deepest mystical and philosophical perceptions. Nevertheless, when a flatly secularized culture has so repressed the deeper perceptions and experience of human experience, these will emerge, in forms sometimes odd and unnerving. Perhaps the soundest tactic of all is to keep trying to get to the question that is being asked in each instance. When traditional doctrinal, moral, and conceptual forms are no longer available as answers, it becomes a matter of learning again what is present but too long unnamed. It could be that there is evidence of a benign conspiracy when deeply felt human values are asserting themselves in various contexts of science, economics, politics, and ecology, to say nothing of religion itself. Such is the case, too, when, in these contexts, experts and amateurs can meet. The experts can find themselves disarmed in the realization that we are all amateurs, both regarding our terrestrial humanity and in relationship to its place in the ever-mysterious universe. Nevertheless, an amateur status in science can find new heart as the wonder of the universe is disclosed in the sophisticated techniques of scientific exploration.

There is evidence of a deeper search for meaning and a desire to learn by heart the movement and form of the universe in which we so uncannily exist. A flatly secularized culture has repressed the deeper perceptions and experience of human consciousness; traditional doctrinal and conceptual forms are no longer available as answers. Hence, the need for an integral ecology.

CHAPTER 3

Ecological Conduct

I N THE INTERESTS of an integral ecology, this chapter considers
four types of response: the pragmatic, the ethical, the aesthetic,
and what we might call "the good intention," or more simply,
contemplation. Note that each attempts to specify what ecology
deals with in its concern for the community of living things on this
planet.[1] The encyclical of Pope Francis, *Laudato Si'*, involves many
types of discourse, ranging from the scientific to the philosophical
and the theological.[2] The Catholic concern for social justice is
a traditional setting for ecological reflection, as concern for our
neighbor broadens into concern for the neighborhood and its
planetary setting. In this regard, science and faith, meaning and
values, action and responsibility must move into a new form of
collaboration. Critical reflection is necessary since science and
technology are not value-free: they embed and promote specific
values in the formation of the human and ecological world. Hence
the need for an integral ecology that is alert to all dimensions of
the problem and open to all sources of wisdom and hope.

THE PRAGMATIC APPROACH

This first approach is the most accessible. It tends, predictably, to be
impatient with any talk of such arcane matters as holistic consciousness, integral ecology, the theology of creation and incarnation, and

the inner ecology of culture itself. The well-intentioned pragmatist might say, "By all means, say your prayers, and love your neighbor; but real action consists in concentrating on recycling and composting, on conserving fossil fuels, on protecting endangered species, in lobbying business and government, in getting a good education program going, and in supporting various activist groups." Such sensible pragmatism focuses on conditions within the environment. It aims to replace a bad environment with a good one so that energy is conserved, the variety of life is preserved, and everything works better.

Despite the energy and expertise of this pragmatic approach, it shelves several radical questions. Since the pragmatic mind confronts issues as problems to be solved, in a vigorous extroversion, it turns to what's wrong *out there*. However, its busy plans and strategic interventions make it unlikely that underlying issues will be noticed *in here*, and diagnosed in relation to a deeply distorted way of life. Pragmatists assume the role of expert problem solvers, acting from outside the living systems they aim to protect. The bias of the pragmatist and the problem solver often hurries past the deeper challenges of intimacy with the other. For this *other* is typically envisaged as a problem awaiting an energetic solution. To talk of complex connections and relationships, let alone the ultimate horizon of surrender, mystery, and the gift of it all, blunts the sharp edge of resolve.

Regrettably, the purely activist approach tends to leave out its best resources, the self that is capable of contemplation, reflection, compassion, and hope. There is no substitute for putting our best selves into the ecological challenge. But such a personal commitment presupposes resources that may not be available. Suddenly to reverse the state of breakdown, or to become conscious of an underlying diseased way of life, are not practical possibilities. By extension, to think of the ecological crisis merely as a technological problem to be solved by better techniques leaves the character of technological culture unexamined. Thus, it is doomed to repeat the old mistakes, even if less lethally. If we still think of reality like a big machine, then we are, at best, engineers; at worst, little cogs within it. Of course, the army of those who are working for better technologies, for a healthier environment, for the conservation of endangered species, and so forth, deserve every commendation and support.

But that is only part of the picture. A deeper involvement of the self is called for; and that emerges in the domain of ethics and the awareness of moral values.

THE ETHICAL APPROACH

On this level, moral values are perceived as the necessary motivation for ecological action. More inclusive forms of the common good, natural law, solidarity, and compassion surface in a shared globally extended conscience. One version of this is the language of rights. We speak of the right to a healthy environment, even the rights *of* a given environment, or of the living beings making it up, such as animals, rain forests, and ocean reefs.[3] However historically odd the language of animal rights and liberation must appear, there is no doubting the genuine, freshly perceived values its expresses.

Still, a certain reserve on the long-term usefulness of rights language is justified. The problem again turns on the peculiar externality of the ecological relationship implied. For example, campaigners for the rights of those others, ranging all the way from native cultures, to animal species such as whales, koalas, or frilled-neck lizards, to biosystems such as ocean reefs and rain forests, can be uncritically secure in their own liberation. To put the matter baldly: all the "others" to be liberated are being offered the freedom already in the possession of the liberators. It is hardly noticed that the ideal of justice presumed in all this is itself rather narrow and distorted. It so often communicates a notion of rights that is militantly adversarial in tone, individualistic in content, and self-assertive and competitive in style. It is born of a mistrust of consensus, uninterested in genuine conversation, and impatient with the complexity of the issues. The malaise of any number of modern democracies provides ample illustration here.

The language of justice, if detached from a gracious worldview, becomes the rigid expression of a violently competitive society. It is not the language of communion, conviviality, mutual belonging, and humble service. A morally ecological language certainly needs to be supported by a renewed sense of justice; but it also needs the energies of an other-directed love. Justice detached from an inclusive sense of the larger common good has been, in fact, the cultural source of our present troubles: it privileges the individual and favors those most able to exploit the system to their advantage. In an imperfect world, one must concede, such a notion still has its point. But if it is tongue-tied when it comes to envisaging a world of communion, of self-dispossession for the sake of the other, so that any ethical concern veers toward a harsh intolerant moralism—we have another version of justice for the few at the expense of the many.

In practice, ethics needs the illumination of the artist and the mystic to support a larger sense of the gift of life in all its forms. Inevitable conflicts must be for the sake of deeper conviviality and greater love. However vulnerable and utopian it will always appear, the supreme value of love is the radically real issue: the love of one's neighbor, the love of the neighborhood; love for one's enemy and loving what is strange, untamed, hitherto unnoticed or even useless; loving it because it exists, given into a world of being and life beyond any calculation, in a holy communion of life and existence within the mystery of creation.

THE AESTHETIC APPROACH

Nor can ecological action be governed simply by aesthetics, at least in the superficial sense of human beings performing the role of planetary landscape gardeners. The destruction of what was once beautiful, or the beauty of what can easily be destroyed, certainly provokes its own powerful reaction. But nature is more than a pleasant ambience: concentrating on beauty alone, even the beauty of all the varied creation of plant and animal life, is not enough. We are leaving ourselves, and a good deal of nature itself, out of the picture. We are seeing ourselves as vacationers, tourists, spectators, park rangers, and landscape gardeners who want to preserve what we imagine has to be a beautiful environment. This can be the subtlest form of ecological insensitivity, in which a weed is anything I have not planted, and a pest is any creature I cannot manage. That is to deny the full given reality of nature in all its variety, including death and decay.

Every beautiful woman has always known that being treated merely as a beautiful object can be a belittling experience. Her essential humanity, including all the negativity and struggle, is repressed, disallowed, or denied. To be treated merely as an aesthetic or sexual object is an insult to her distinctive personality with its aspirations to freedom, relationships, and fullness of life. Then, there is another perspective, since beauty is notoriously in the eye of the beholder. For some, an old wharf in a city harbor is an eyesore obscuring the natural shore. For others, it is a thing of beauty, a historical part of the place, something to be cherished, and in the event, defended. When ecological concerns focus only on maintaining a pleasing environment, debates on what should be treasured or removed collapse into a clash on individual tastes.

In contrast, a more realistic ecological approach needs a larger horizon. Its standpoint is openness to the mystery of nature in all its grandeur, beauty, particularity, struggle, and mortality. The actions of integral ecological activity arise from intimate receptivity to the whole as something to belong to, live with, work for, and yield to; yet in a way that allows for the distinctive contribution that human beings bring to the realm of nature.

Though ecological action is not only a matter of aesthetics, it can be guided by the activity of artists and the work of artistic creation.[4] Artists have a respectful and receptive working relationship to their materials. Within the given limits of stone, paint, tonal scale, or physical movement, a creative interaction occurs. A new form is educed, as reality is illumined by the human creative act. Matter is freshly imagined, released to a new intensity of existence in a new form of embodiment.

Such an approach allows for the creative activity of the human, but only within given limits and conditions. To this degree, there is a certain corealization of artist and artwork, as nature plays itself out through artistic imagination into life-nourishing beauty.[5] Human activity is the medium by which nature can be elevated to a new form. In human imagination, nature stands ready to receive the inexhaustible, the surprising, a revelation. Through art, nature touches on the intimations of the transcendent. This approach bears some analogy to the venerable medieval conviction of grace healing, perfecting, and elevating nature. Here, grace is understood as the loving excess of divine creativity, and nature is the creativity of human potential. In an ecological application, the human can be understood to be called by grace to embrace the larger domain of nature as a gift—thus, to heal, preserve, perfect, and elevate it. In this theological tradition, grace and nature are not identical, nor does grace destroy nature, for grace transforms human nature by liberating it to attain to the union with God that it naturally seeks.

In the ecological context, we can locate this theological axiom at a more preliminary stage: as God is the source of all gifts to the human, the human itself can come as a gift to the whole of nature. In this symbiosis and synergy, human action maintains its own initiative and uniqueness in the exercise of creativity and freedom. In that way, the human comes to nature as a transforming gift. But that does not mean that the human can destroy nature. The human is meant to be a healing and preserving grace for all the natural world. But there is a transformative moment of grace in that the human "elevates" nature, by liberating it to a new fullness of communion and integrity. When nature is seen, neither primarily as a philosophical notion, nor as restricted to the domain of human sinfulness or capability, but rather as a living, interrelated system of life on this planet, a new set of correlations is called for.

In summary, a purely pragmatic relationship is not enough, for it would leave too much unexamined. When the human agent is unaffected by a radical conversion of some kind, ecological proposals risk being merely the projection of an unexamined cultural status quo. Something deeper is required. Nor is it merely a matter of a more explicit ethical stance: without an ongoing effort to understand the larger context and to make room for a more comprehensive sense of the common good in all its attractive and transcendent implications, ethics soon collapses into oppressive moralism. Nor is it simply a matter of a new aesthetic. Not everything is beautiful; and life has piercing tragedies. The problem of evil remains.

Nonetheless, a model of artistic action suggests something of the transformative influence of the human within the whole natural order, particularly when that, in turn, is set within the presence and action of the Creator Spirit. The resources and goal of transformation reach their richest Christian expression only when set within the transforming experience of universal love.

CONTEMPLATION: INDWELLING CREATION

How does the contemplative dynamism of faith, hope, and love affect the realism of ecological relationships? Through the "theological virtues," the believer dwells in the universe as God's creation, to contemplate it, however dimly or inchoatively, in its radically mysterious wholeness.

First, faith, informed by love, works on the highest level of communal self-realization. Essentially, at the deepest roots of consciousness, we are already involved with the ultimate mystery of our existence. Some speak of "a pre-religious love-affair with God," however unnamed or unknown as such.[6] This is to say that the movement of consciousness is a living search for the ultimate fulfillment of our relational being. It unfolds within a horizon of ultimacy. What theology termed "a natural desire to see God," or a desire for beatitude, recent thinkers express in more psychological terms as the restless intentionality of the mind's search for meaning and the ultimate worth of all we most value. To be human is to be a meaning-making, truth-beholden, value-drawn being. As Lonergan states in his lapidary manner, "Man's transcendental subjectivity is mutilated or abolished, unless he is stretching forth toward the intelligible, the unconditioned, the good of value...our native orientation to the divine."[7] To what degree can this "native orientation to the divine" inform the relationships involved in an integral ecology? A relational quality of consciousness involved.

Second, the quality referred to is love—the *agape* of the New Testament, the *caritas* of the Catholic tradition. Though this is a distinctively Christian formulation, such love is understood to be a universal gift, however different religious traditions might express it. The original overture of human consciousness to the ultimate is kindled into intimacy through the gift of God (Rom 5:5; 1 John 4:7–12). Through the gift of love, human consciousness homes to its final goal, and indwells a world radically transformed.

Such fulfillment registers in the converted mind and heart as transcendent peace and freedom. Yet it comes within the dynamics and texture of contemporary culture. While it focuses on the ultimate, its basis can indeed be broadened, deepened, and enriched to include ecological concerns and commitments.

Contemplative indwelling in the world through love is experienced as relational and dynamic.[8] For it is manifest as a transition from isolation and emptiness to the connectedness and plenitude of communion with life in all its manifestations. Self-surrender to God is stimulating on earth a new range of the desires, fears, joys, and sorrows, discernment of values, decisions, and activity, as loving collaboration with the God of creation. It is an expansion of loving God and of all in God. When one loves God "with all your heart, and with all your soul, and with all your mind, and with all your strength" (Mark 12:30), the human heart (see Rom 5:5), reaches beyond family and friends to embrace all creation. The emerging ecological consciousness can share the conviction of St. Paul that "neither death, nor life…nor things present, nor things to come, nor powers, nor height, nor depth, nor anything else in all creation, will be able to separate us from the love of God in Christ Jesus our Lord" (Rom 8:38–39).[9]

As nothing in all creation can separate us from the loving source of our existence, nothing is more calculated to link us with that creation in a joyous participative companionship. It is likened to falling in love with God within the universe of divine creation, in all its variety and in all its groaning generativity, in deep collaboration with the Creator Spirit.

In summary: the Christian experience of the communion of life has three features.[10] First, there is an immediate intimacy with the all-inclusive mystery. This fundamental simplicity is always in tension with the complex mediations of culture and religious tradition. Such mediations constitute an immense and complex superstructure, articulated in word and ritual, institution and law, spiritual counsel and moral persuasion, along with all the variety of theologies and scientific and philosophical theories, historical narrative, traditions, and worldviews. But through all these and reaching beyond them, faith connects with the inexpressible and ultimately inclusive realm of life and love. It leads to what is often invoked as "learned ignorance" taking consciousness beyond all formulations, even those most treasured in the tradition. Faith lives in the presence of the one surpassing reality, for which there are no adequate words. Even the words *reality* and *cause* are limited by their earth-bound significance. Mystics speak of inhaling the perfume of the divinity, of being wounded, inflamed, possessed by it, even while being unable to name it. The range of faith exceeds all other kinds of knowing. Rather matter-of-factly, St. Thomas Aquinas asserts, "The act of the believer does not terminate at a statement [about God] but at the Reality."[11] In tension with the various mediations of belief, of theology, and all other kinds of knowing, the mystical contact of faith cherishes its dark intimacy with the divine. A relevant point is that God is never to be fitted into a system as a factor or a process, but is the focus in which everything is centered, the realm of ultimate communion, the breath or atmosphere vitalizing all existence.

Second is the quality of *interiority*. This mode of consciousness stands in tension with common sense apprehensions of the world in which God is thought of as "up there," a big agent in the governing of the world, or a big "thing" within it. Furthermore, it is another dimension compared to the intellectual world of theory, and its theological and philosophical systems. For the life of faith engages the whole being from the depths of the heart, and not just intelligence or moral inclination or technical know-how. In familiar biblical and spiritual discourse, God dwells in the heart of the mystic and the mystic dwells in God. The mysticism of faith is not primarily busy in the articulation of a system or in making a synthesis. It lives in a presence, dwelling in it, surrendering to it. It is the eminent example of knowing by the heart, when "the heart has its reasons which reason itself does not know" (Pascal). To that degree, the dimension of interiority leads to a knowledge of familiarity, of the immersion of the whole self in the holy wholeness of things.

Third, the mystical orientation of faith is characterized by a *universal* and unrestricted scope. It lives from its own inherent excess. Here, too, as noted earlier, the range of faith surpasses the particularities of doctrinal, theological, or moral contexts. It breathes and "has been groaning" (Rom 8:18–28) in the mystery of the Holy Spirit[12] who inspires hope for a wholeness that cannot be thought, imagined, or named. The experience of faith, in its immediate, interior integrity, is that of an inexpressible excess. Though such consciousness is marked by all the groaning limitations of obscurity, incompleteness, and tension, it does not terminate in either absurdity or ultimate futility. Its universe is not a vast *reductio ad absurdum*. The basic character of its unfolding is that of surrender and adoration. It works more as a *reductio in mysterium*, as all things are led back to the original and abiding mystery at work in everything and everyone.

CONCLUSION

Integral ecology is about becoming *someone* in mind, heart, and imagination, and doing *something* in action, as a participant in a global conversion. Let us note just seven matters that affect the style of integral ecology.

Language

First, there is the question of language. If we intend to speak in a language that might help a global ecological conversation on basic ethical responsibilities and common values, our language cannot be limited to the terms of a specific religion, philosophy, culture, language group, or scientific specialization. While there are rich resources in the Catholic approach to an integral ecology, they need to be critically transposed to meet the concerns of the entire world, with its varied cultural perspectives. Faith may provide the motivation to engage in the widest possible moral dialogue, but it does not supply the terms. It does not automatically speak a common language able to name the values of nature, justice, decency, freedom, community, cosmic harmony, and the kind of self-realization prized in the diverse cultures. Consequently, an integral ecology must be not only sensitive to language, but creative in its communications, as in poetry, song, and all the arts.

Humanity

An integral ecology cannot presume that everyone who might participate in the action or contemplation here described is religious, let alone Christian. However, there is a valuable Pauline counsel for Church leaders and thinkers in their dialogue with the larger world. St. Paul expresses his absolute commitment to the crucified and risen Christ and the hope that this entails:

> I regard everything as loss because of the surpassing value of knowing Christ Jesus my Lord. For his sake I have suffered the loss of all things, and I regard them as rubbish, in order that I may gain Christ. (Phil 3:8)

Consequently, we might not expect that Paul would have much time for ecology! But a few verses later, he opens a window into the wide world of common values:

> Whatever is true, whatever is honorable, whatever is just, whatever is pure, whatever is pleasing, whatever is commendable, if there is any excellence and if there is anything worthy of praise, think about these things. (Phil 4:8)

Here, Paul is appealing to the moral imperative inherent in being a member of the human race. Whatever the problems and conflicts, the sense of an ecology of values makes possible a discussion of what constitutes the communion of planetary life in terms of nature. Nature is the field of communication in which we identify one another—and all living things—as belonging in the natural world within a web of codependent and, for humans, of moral consciousness. In this context, nature is both what all are born with, and born into, as well as being a program of mutual responsibility.

Connaturality

Participating in nature through an integral ecology suggests an attraction, however implicit, toward the good of all that is beyond all restrictions. And yet there is an "excess" to be found in spiritual experience of a more contemplative kind. It sets all natures and responsibilities in a context of collaboration with the creative will and purpose working throughout the universe—however this may be named. It can be described as a contemplative sense of nature as a communion of life. To this degree, an integral ecology inspires what, in the vocabulary of the Thomistic tradition, was termed "connaturality." It suggests intimate attunement of the human to the whole of creation, and above all, to the creative source of all.

Cosmic

In the background of discussions relating to integral ecology, there is a growing awareness of the cosmic story of planet Earth, and the emergence of human nature and the entire ecologically interacting web of natures in the "natural world," within an uncanny evolutionary history spanning the immensity of space and time. Human nature and all of nature can now situate itself within a cosmic 14 billion-year prehistory.[13] To be aware of the uncanny emergence of the cosmos, and of the singularity of life on this planet, is to live with a new sense of proportion. Whatever our national, ethnic, cultural, or religious differences, we have a common origin within an unimaginably immense and fecund cosmic process. Given the sheer contingency of our existence, despite the infinitesimal insignificance of our physical being in the physical universe, human consciousness has a unique capacity to ask the big questions: What is the significance of human existence? How does human nature belong to all natures, and how do we belong together? How should we collaborate to bring a distinctively human contribution to the history of life in which we participate?

New Capabilities

In today's global experience, the sense of our common human emergence is accompanied by new human capacities. The astonishing developments in electronic communications have brought a new intensity and immediacy into human contact—and even to the wonders and intricacies of nature itself, as Sir David Attenborough so magnificently brings to our attention. It is as though our senses have been immeasurably extended. Everyone is newly embodied in an electronic network of communication of enormous potential for social interaction, culture, business, and integral ecology. From this point of view, human nature is less a philosophical abstraction and more something being actualized in an interface *with all nature*. Human existence is necessarily coexistence within the realm of nature, and, indeed, depends on the biophysical world for its survival. For its part, human intelligence and freedom can be understood as a dimension of the creativity and adaptability of nature as a whole in sustaining life in all its forms.

Inner Ecology

The conflicts and problems that arise point to the need of some integrating ecology of values. The environmental crisis is not unrelated to the ecology of human culture and its ability to respect a hierarchy of values—physical, biological, vital (health), political, economic, cultural, and religious—in their dynamic confluence within an integral ecology.

As for the "global" context, it is not enough to keep repeating the now worn-out metaphor of the "global village" in which a privileged minority of the world's people consume most of its produce, own most of the natural resources, and control the means of production. In its best connotation, the global context connotes a newly emerging stage in world history.

Animality

Even when adverting to the evolutionary emergence of nature and its ecology, as humans, we can be so "spiritual" in our sense of identity as to become oblivious of the generic "animality" of the human condition. We are not "disembodied intelligences tentatively considering possible incarnations," but concretely embodied human beings on planet Earth.[14] Our capacities to bond, to care for our young, to feel for the entire community of terrestrial life, are all rooted in our evolutionary animal nature. As Mary Midgley observes, "We are not just like animals; we *are* animals."[15] Our kinship with the animal realm offsets any ethereal sentiment of individual existence and global belonging impatient with the inherent limitations of each. Specific feelings and actual kinds of bonding are "given" in ways that demand respect. Neither interpersonal relations nor religiously inspired universal love can afford to bypass a natural ordering of relationships—as Stephen Pope has convincingly shown.[16] By owning our ecological place in an evolutionary biological world, we are less inclined to think of the human self as a free-floating consciousness. Our present responsibilities have a biologically based emotional constitution. They are shaped in a specific direction by the genesis of nature. There are "givens" in the human constitution; and these conditions precede freedom, never to be repudiated unless at the cost of denaturing ourselves in a fundamental manner. In sexuality, for instance, neither culture nor a person-centered spirituality is the only consideration. Primary relationships to family, friends, community, society, and to the earth itself, need to be recognized in their particularity as priorities in our concerns. We belong to the whole human family through a specific family. We enter the global community of planet Earth by being connected to a special place and time. Self-transcendence is possible only by way of the given limits and connections. Though we are naturally and instinctually bonded to our own species, our common animal descent on this planet has bred into us an innate affective sense of belonging to the whole terrestrial community of life, and responsibility for it.

Integral ecology is a way of appreciating the world in its heights and depths. It is at once a contemplative dwelling in the mystery of the world, and a way of humbly relating to it. With this in mind, let's now explore the idea of consciously indwelling the gift of creation.

CHAPTER 4

Indwelling Creation

I N REFLECTING ON the Creator, creation, and ecology from
the perspective of human consciousness, our aim is to better
interiorize our sense of the presence of God and extend the
possibility of dialogue. The emphases are on our experience, the
phenomenon of consciousness, and the intentionality of our
knowing and valuing. In this respect, we focus on experience
of consciousness itself in order to intensify the ecological sense
of dwelling in creation and dwelling in God. In terms of an
integral ecology, questions arise as to the meaning of ecology
and our human place within it. It is important, therefore, not to
paint ourselves into a corner, or saw off the branch in which our
conscious humanity is sitting. To do this, we must first consider
the all-inclusive character of creation.

ALL-INCLUSIVE CREATION

For instance, if we imagine creation as a noun signifying a big
objective totality produced by the Creator, we naturally tend to
envisage it as something to which we are oddly extrinsic. Our
thinking and feeling, praying, desiring, exploring, and creating are
merely a faint mode of being, ghosting the objective reality of the
universe, but not really a contributing part of the living whole.
Creation, the physical universe, and the interactions of a living

ecology are imagined as objectively given and, at best, subject to human inspection and scientific analysis.

Human Consciousness

There is something missing from such a perspective, namely, the phenomenon of consciousness itself. Human consciousness is an intrinsic feature of being human. It is, too, an inward dimension of creation itself through which God's creation becomes known and appreciated. Consciousness is not, therefore, an ethereal idea or an imaginary "ghosting" of reality, but a primal experience accessible in every act and moment of our lives.

Consciousness can be described as multileveled self-presence. It occurs in different registers, in every act of sensing, imagining, questioning, understanding, judging, deciding, acting, loving, and contemplating. In this inward dimension, we act, and reality reveals itself. We are not, therefore, detached spectators looking at what is somehow already "out there." Rather, our consciousness is the site in which what is to be known is given to sense, imagination, and intelligence. It thereby provokes questions as to what is, or might be, the case. In other words, objectivity, even of the highest scientific kind, can never be attained by pretending that there is not *someone* who does the knowing. Human consciousness is always in the picture, and, for that matter, consciously on the line regarding its own integrity.

Human consciousness, in all its modes and dynamics—intellectual, moral, aesthetic, religious, and so on—needs to be appreciated as an intrinsic feature of reality if we are to have a true sense of creation. Consciousness is disclosed as it accompanies and grows our acts of sensing, imagining, questioning, judging, and deciding. It intensifies and expands as we stand in wonder and contemplate the mystery of it all. In this sense, it is the inward dimension of how reality reveals itself. According to an ancient insight, the mind knowing reality and reality known are one.

For those who might fear that such a suggestion is dangerously subjective, we concede that subjectivity is indeed dangerous, that is, when it is no more than *subjectivism*, as though the real and the true are merely projections of our own feelings, imaginations, or bright ideas. In contrast, the only way to be genuinely objective is through the conscious unfolding of our capacities to sense, imagine, understand, and weigh the evidence. We can never be so objective as to leave out the activities of the knowing subject, but that includes the felt impulse to go beyond ourselves, out of ourselves, into the awesome otherness of all that is, with which we coexist on this planet and in this universe.

The Value of Objectivity

This is not to suggest that any one finite mind comprehends the whole, for our capacities are always limited, and our limited knowledge is never so absolute that no further questions remain. Hence, knowledge can only advance through collaboration with countless others, each witnessing to the integrity of their respective finite attainments in what they have judged to be meaningful, true, and good. Knowledge grows, no matter what the cost to personal expectations, preferences, and ingrained prejudices; collaboration becomes possible, and history progress.

It would be an odd situation, then, to screen out of the picture what is most obvious, namely the consciousness in which the picture appears in the first place. Attention to the phenomenon of consciousness cannot be deferred to the possibility of some future discovery of the interaction of the brain's neurons. Consciousness is the most obvious datum, and without it no investigation could proceed. There is an odd blind spot in the materialist creed: a denial of the existence of God has a strange parallel in the denial of the existence of the conscious self![1] After all, the affirmation of the real objective order is the outcome of our human conscious creativity in all its modes. It is true that the universe is more than an ensemble of human acts of understanding, or more than the manifestation of human minds. But neither can it be known without them.

We have so far been, in effect, questioning "the myth of objectivity" that imagines that objectivity can be abstracted from human consciousness or be possible without it. The genuine thrust to objectivity is something quite different. If human consciousness closed itself against the imperative of being objective, it would necessarily collapse into solipsism. The world draws us out of ourselves; and only by allowing ourselves to be taken beyond the narrow confines of a habitat or culture can the self expand to its limitless proportions: Aristotle and Aquinas agree that the human soul is in some measure open to everything (*anima est quodammodo omnia*). In fact, Aquinas, following Aristotle on this point, finds in the objective consideration of nature a healthy corrective to a diseased or distorted subjectivity. In the "book of creation," he notes that there are so many creatures "that deliver the truth without falsehood. Wherefore Aristotle, when asked whence it was that he had his admirable learning, replied, 'From things which do not know how to lie.'"[2]

The bracing value of objectivity is evident in Aquinas's confident intellectual commitment to "the things that do not know how to lie."[3] The challenge today is to reappraise the seemingly simple requirement of being objective. It demands an integration of the subjective dynamics of the mind in the process of being objective. It is not enough to downplay the subjective as the area where lying is possible, through deceit, bias, and foolishness. But a vital insight occurs when one notices that any objective statement about what is the case is the complex outcome of the conscious drive to self-transcendence. We need to focus on what is given, questioning its meaning, and weigh the evidence, to arrive at a responsible, however conditional, true statement. Lonergan's axiom applies: "Genuine objectivity is the fruit of authentic subjectivity."[4] Subjectivity is authentic when the subject concerned is present to itself precisely as responding to all the demands of reality. To know any truth, one must attend to all the pertinent data, refine one's sensibilities, vitalize one's imagination, ask the unwelcome questions, consider the possible answers in broad and differentiated fields of meaning, and ponder the emerging evidence in a disinterested commitment to truth. This enables the subject finally to take its place as a trustworthy agent in the vast collaborative exercise of illuminating the manifold mystery of existence and of forming a more human world.

From Consciousness to Soul

In genuine scientific objectivity, the activities of sensing, imagining, questioning, reflecting, and deciding are all present. But the typically overlooked domain of data to be considered is the data of consciousness itself, above all, the consciousness of scientists themselves in their acts of understanding. The experience of intelligence is not irrelevant. More deeply, awareness of the dynamics of intellectual activity leads to a reevaluation, within the experience of exploring the universe, of what was once simply called "soul," "spirit," "mind," or "heart." Aquinas considered that "the human soul understands itself by its understanding, which is its proper act, perfectly demonstrating its power and nature."[5] A modern scientist observes,

> We must try once again to experience the human soul as soul, and not just a buzz of bioelectricity; the human will as will, and not just a surge of hormones; the human heart not as a fibrous sticky pump, but as the metaphoric organ of understanding.[6]

There is deep spiritual significance in recovering the classic philosophical sense of the "soul" as the metaphysical expression of human subjectivity in a more contemporary mode.[7] It opens the question of God in the most intimate fashion. Aquinas, early in his career, wrote as he reflected on the human soul as the most mysterious entity within creation, "God is the greatest of all goods and more proper to each one than anything else can be because he is closer to the soul than the soul is to itself."[8]

The Question of God

Certainly, the question of God can never be satisfactorily raised if science methodically excludes from its considerations scientists themselves, as they experience their own intelligently conscious activities. Out of that experience of intelligence and responsibility, there can arise the intimation of God.[9] It will not be a God as a patriarchal projection, nor as a temporary stopgap, nor as a cosmic force, not as primeval matter or universal order; but God as the ecstatic intelligence and love that gives rise to the universe in which intelligent and responsive selves can operate. God is Light, unrestricted intelligence; and the human mind is a participation in that light, as it progressively elucidates what is, and grows in responsibility with a concern for what should be.

In this way, the experience of God can occur far more intimately than was the case in the classical form of the question, which pivoted on the insight that no existent reality, nor all such realities taken together, could be the explanation of why anything or everything existed. The objective inexplicable reality of the world was thus the starting point for proving the existence of the Creator, as first cause, end, supreme perfection, and so forth.

The trouble with this approach is that it no longer poses the question of the Creator God intimately enough. Too often, the universe of reality was considered as though the human mind were some neutral observer, a spectator, existing in another realm, somehow outside the whole emergent process. To repeat: our conscious experiences of observing, imagining, understanding, and valuing are dimensions of the actual universe. These activities are the aspects of creation with which we are most familiar. They make the question of creation freshly and piercingly intimate. It is a question posed from within. It is foreshadowed in the very activity of knowing, by the very fact that everything is in principle intelligible. The character of the universe is felt in the ultimate attractiveness of the values of truth, goodness, justice, and compassion. In our explorations, by including the experience of wondering, knowing, and responsible selves, we arrive at a sense of being beholden to an "Other," the source, enablement, and fulfillment of the thrust to self-transcendence. We find ourselves, not at the controlling center of the universe, but as participating in its limitless mystery.

Wittgenstein ruminated on the fact that there is anything at all; Einstein marveled at the intelligibility of the universe. Rilke recommended that poets be "bees of invisible," and another poet, Judith Wright, felt in her whole being a consonance with universal energies: "But who wants to be a mere onlooker? Every cell of me / has been pierced through by plunging intergalactic messages."[10]

More specifically, we can reflect on ourselves, as caught up and carried along in a great cosmic unfolding, precisely as it presents us with ourselves in this actual world. As human creatures, our given role is to participate in the universe, celebrate its varied wonder, contribute to its direction in love, and yield to its promise in hope. We can come to an ecological awareness, as relationally located in the web and wave of cosmic realities that nourish body, mind, and heart. The world shimmers with intelligibility in our minds, thrills with value in our hearts, and bursts into our imagination with its beauty. At that moment, we are not dispassionate observers, but ecstatic participants. To quote Judith Wright again:

> While I'm in my five senses
> they send me spinning
> all sounds and silences,
> all shape and colour
> as thread for that weaver,
> whose web within me growing
> follows beyond my knowing
> some pattern sprung from nothing—
> a rhythm that dances
> and is not mine.[11]

And then, as the theologian Robert Faricy states,

> When the concept of the human spirit is understood... as the mode of consciousness in which the individual feels connected to the cosmos as a whole, it becomes clear that ecological awareness is truly spiritual. Indeed the idea of the individual being linked to the cosmos is expressed in the Latin root of the word, religion, *religare* ("to bind strongly") as well as the Sanskrit *yoga* which means union.[12]

Creation and Collaboration

The question of creation is, then, an area where deeply methodological questions regarding the collaborative character of human knowledge are posed. Is there a way of respecting the complete range of the human exploration of meaning, truth, and goodness?[13] There is no point in talking about creation and the Creator of all—including the human mind and heart—if some of the data are declared inadmissible, above all the datum, the "given," of our own conscious selves. After all, we are each alive, conscious, plunged ecstatically into a world of daily meaning, communication, and responsibility. In that world, love brings forth what is best in our lives, just as beauty in art or nature continually refreshes our perceptions of the uncanny gift of existence.

This may sound too broad or obscurantist to the hard-nosed scientist. I have not the slightest intention of denying the value of scientific research. By implying that the totality of reality eludes any exclusively scientific method, I am attempting to locate scientific method in a larger field of human experience and exploration. Indeed, I think that the theology of creation points to a background theme in which all our diverse human creativities can improvise their variations as part of the symphony of reality. The scientist and philosopher Michael Polanyi, by pointing to the manifold and dynamic structure of human knowing, suggests possibilities of generous collaboration between science, philosophy, and theology—even if it still remains a remote ideal:

> Admittedly, religious conversion commits our whole person and changes our whole being in a way that an expansion of our natural knowledge does not do. But once the dynamics of knowing are recognised as the dominant principle of knowledge, the difference appears only as one of degree....It establishes a continuous ascent from our less personal knowing of inanimate matter to our convivial knowing of living beings and beyond this to knowing our responsible fellow men. Such I believe is the true transition from the sciences to the humanities, and also from our knowing the laws of nature to our knowing the person of God.[14]

To admit, therefore, different degrees or levels of an increasingly personal knowing is to experience the question of creation and its Creator as inscribed into the dynamics of self-transcending, personal being. It helps frame questions such as the following:

- What is the creativity that has sustained and moved forward the evolutionary self-transcendence of the universe?
- What is the light in which we explore the universe and come to understand it to some degree?
- What is the primordial unity in which this given totality is a "uni-verse," a coexistence, even a communion that has enabled the chaos of atoms and molecules,

of life forms and consciousness, of relationships and processes, to emerge as we contemplate it, in awe and responsibility, at this present moment?[15]

We now turn to the creative activity of God.

GOD CREATING

Then there is the question of *creation* as a verb. Either for religious or philosophical reasons, we might propose that creation is an original and continuing divine activity, and may be imagined as a superior kind of activity. The essential jolt to this imaginative fallacy was traditionally supplied by the addition of a mysterious phrase: God creates "out of nothing," *ex nihilo sui et subjecti*. The divine creative act presupposes nothing already in existence—no raw material; no chain of events; no previous dispositions.[16] God is not conditioned by anything already in existence. There is nothing *there*—outside the divine act—that God somehow uses "to make the world." The imagination, however devout, cannot quite handle that. It tends inescapably to imagine God as the biggest actor in a world of doers and movers. It tends to locate God, perhaps like a big angel, an agency, in a cosmos of causes, principles, and energies. In contrast is the notion of the divine creative act, not as one category of causing, doing, or deciding, but as a transcendent, therefore unimaginable, mode of causing things to be and to act. The Creator acts in the acting of everything, and causes in the causality of every agent. Such a notion of creation strains the imagination. We need to recognize that we are dealing with radical mystery, unlike anything in the world of doing and causing. God is the ungraspable ground and energy of all being and acting. But first we must dwell once more on what we mean by "God."[17]

Converging Approaches to God

It is tempting to discuss creation without using the time-(dis?) honored word *God*. The biblical and philosophical traditions that have formed Christian understanding of creation know other terms such as "Word," "Light," "Spirit," "Source," "Life," "Love," "Being" (note, "Being" is a *verb*, as in the Thomistic, *Ipsum Esse*—literally, "Sheer *To-Be*"), "limitless Act" (i.e., the *Actus Purus* of Western philosophic tradition), "ultimate reality," "fount of being," "final good," "first cause," and many others.

Often, discussion is blocked by the emotional fixations, fantastic distortions, and conceptual straitjackets with which a variety of cultural conflicts have imbued this one word, *God*. Nonetheless, we must persevere with it. After all, it does not let us escape from the unredeemed elements in our history. Nonetheless, other terms are available. In dealing with the mystery that transcends human language, we need to keep in play the whole vocabulary, even as we maintain the reverent restraint so characteristic of the Jewish tradition in which the personal name of God was seldom written or pronounced.

The real problem, however, is not with words, be they marks on a page or vibrations of sound. It resides, rather, in how these terms are used, and in what they are to mean. For the believer, the first and fundamental notion of God is found in an orientation to that limitless, living fullness of being and goodness that, alone, in the deepest sense of the traditional term, "saves our souls." In more contemporary language, the sense of God is intimated as that which fulfills the movement toward self-transcendence. The meaning of God is, as it were, progressively anticipated in our searching. It is felt as an attraction toward the ultimate and unconditioned meaning, truth, beauty, value, love, and mercy, reaching beyond ourselves, and upward to what the world cannot give. Faith occurs when our searching existence throughout history is met with a divine self-disclosure. To believe in this way is to recognize that God is not indifferent to our seeking, but is revealed in the words of the prophets, in the wisdom of the holy ones, in the word of sacred scriptures, in the coming of Christ.

The meaning of *God* is forged within the furnace of history, as idolatrous projections are undermined, and the demons that infest individuals or societies are exorcised.[18] But more than anything else, the meaning of God comes as a gift, indeed as a self-giving on the part of the Creator—to the extreme of entering into suffering humanity: the Word became flesh and dwelt among us. Though God may "mean the world," words fail and are in a continual process of translation. Faith, in its anticipation of life to the full, might use sensory language to name, in some analogical manner, how it sees or hears or touches or tastes the reality of God. In self-surrender and adoration, it might have a vivid sense of the unknown, ever-attractive mystery. In prayer, God is the silence in which all words fall away, the darkness where our brightest ideas fade in the radiance of another light, the all-welcoming Love in which our restless hearts come home. If words can be spoken, God is first of all an invocable, all-relational "You," before the objectifications of "It" or "He" come into play.

Failing to recognize the anticipatory, ongoing character of the meaning of *God* makes dialogue with the reverently agnostic all but impossible, be they scientists or meditative searchers. The result is all too often a collision of congealed concepts and a struggle between disciplines defending their respective borders. In this competitive situation, the scientifically articulated version of reality is taken to be sophisticated, while the religious notion is deemed naïve. This problem continually crops up in the confrontation between the materialist creed of reductive scientism and religious creeds of unthinking faith. It is necessary to keep in mind the strong tradition of biblical agnosticism as it recognizes that God is not yet seen "face to face," and that God "no one has ever seen" (John 1:18). Even though God is the object of our love and faith and hope, the mystery is disclosed only in a progressive darkness.[19] With the shattering of our idols, be they erected by our feelings, need for security, intellectual systems, faith is a liberation in its surrender to the original and ultimate mystery so as neither to grasp or contain it.

There is another pertinent point. Faith comes to believe in the Creator, not because it first believes in creation. Rather, believers speak of creation because, however obscurely, they have come to know the One who alone can create. Admittedly, in the religious domain, there is an undifferentiated affirmation of Creator and creation before philosophical, historical, or scientific questions are asked. As contexts develop, the creation question is framed to meet the demands of different mentalities evident in all the varieties of philosophy and psychology, scientific method or aesthetic sensibilities, evolutionary biology and quantum physics. If faith is to seek further understanding, it must move through many contexts and encounter many different mentalities if, in the end, it is to mature to its full intellectual, ethical, and spiritual potential.

Those who have attained a highly theoretical or scientific mentality approach the question of the explanation of the universe in a form quite different from those who have a specifically spiritual or religious standpoint. These latter tend to pose the question in terms of a prior faith, as it seeks further understanding of how God is, acts, and is revealed in the manifold of a created universe. Scientists, however, pursue their explorations by way of experiment, extrapolation, and hypothesis regarding the specific and tightly controlled band of data in, for example, physics or biology. They deal with the most probable explanation of the data under consideration in the expectation of arriving at more theory. The experience of searching is so vivid to the scientific mentality that scientists might find themselves suggesting that religious believers must wait on their findings before any belief regarding creation can be judged legitimate. Only when all the evidence is in, the scientist might argue, can God—understood within some philosophical, theological, or aesthetic tradition—be reasonably affirmed.

The features of an inevitable and deeply confusing clash of views are clear. On the one hand, those who freely adore the ultimate mystery disclosed to their faith as the source and goal of all, are dismissed as "simple believers," conventionally "religious" because they know no better. On the other hand, believers who might legitimately rejoice in an intimacy with the divine Ground of creation can often lag beyond in terms of intellectual development, especially if respect for critical intelligence has never been part of their way to God. Through lack of leisure, or training, or commitment, to say nothing of suspicion, fear, or laziness, they can be unfamiliar with the explorative value of thought, be it in theology, philosophy, or science. To them, the religious sense of creation is in danger of being replaced by some purely human method, from whose esoteric procedures they are barred. They may feel that the ultimate and universal reach of their faith is called to surrender to a sophisticated elite presiding over the secrets of the universe. Believers feel thus required to become less believers in God, and to be more believing in what scientists proclaim.

In some ways, theologians can become dialogically lazy. After all, the 1913 edition of the *Catholic Encyclopedia* serenely observed,

"The gist of the theory of evolution as a scientific hypothesis...is in perfect agreement with the Christian conception of the universe; for Scripture does not tell us in what form the present species of plants and of animals were originally created by God." This is a time Catholics can be grateful for the philosophical component in their tradition. Nevertheless, Protestant communities, entirely admirable in their commitment of faith, cannot avoid a certain crisis when faith suddenly begins to give rise to metaphysical and epistemological questions, especially in order to meet the challenge of atheism. (Richard Dawkins's dogmatic atheism seems rather tired now after Alister McGrath's devastating critique.[20])

A Generous Biblical Space

We must wonder at the extent to which the neglect of the following biblical remark has left religious thought somewhat impoverished and awkward when it comes to face the great evolutionary and cosmic questions of today. The biblical sage reflects on various kinds of wisdom. For some, the "scientists" of the day,

> were unable from the good things that are seen to
> know the one who exists,
> nor did they recognize the artisan while paying heed to
> his works;
> but they supposed that either fire or wind or swift air,
> or the circle of the stars, or turbulent water,
> or the luminaries of heaven were gods that rule the
> world.
> If through delight in the beauty of these things people
> assumed them to be gods,
> let them know how much better than these is their
> Lord,
> for the author of beauty created them.
> And if people were amazed at their power and working,
> let them perceive from them
> how much more powerful is the one who formed
> them.
> For from the greatness and beauty of created things
> comes a corresponding perception of their Creator.

Yet these people are little to be blamed,
for perhaps they go astray
while seeking God and desiring to find him.
For while they live among his works, they keep
    searching,
and they trust in what they see, because the things that
    are seen are beautiful.
Yet again, not even they are to be excused;
for if they had the power to know so much
that they could investigate the world,
how did they fail to find sooner the Lord of these
    things?

(Wis 13:1–9)

Today "the good things that are seen" have been immeasurably extended. The magnitude of the energies and the infinitesimal intricacies of pattern and design are so fascinating, and so subversive of former visions of reality, that scientific language verges on the religious and the poetic in its effort to express the numinous value of the cosmos it celebrates. For on a purely scientific level, a new enchantment with the beauty and wonder of the cosmos is apparent. Little wonder that there are those who feel they have discovered "the gods that rule the world." In comparison, the God of traditional faith seems little more than a naïve projection.

Whatever the case, we find ourselves in an exuberant Babel of languages. Different mindsets and different methods seek to name the ultimate, and new holistic outlooks try to overcome former antagonistic perceptions of science and religion. Still, the biblical sage graciously admits that those who prefer the wonders of creation to the wonder of the Creator are "little to be blamed." The beauty of life on earth, the uncanny complexity of the universe invites into a further search for ultimate explanation of all explanations.

And yet there remains the possibility of stopping short: "How did they fail to find sooner the Lord of these things?" Further questioning can be silenced by a refusal to think further and to allow for what we have been calling an "integral ecology." The eminent physicist Werner Heisenberg wrote with exemplary openness of mind, "Although I am convinced that scientific truth is unassailable in its own field, I never found it possible to dismiss the content

70

of religious thinking....Thus, in the course of my life, I have been repeatedly compelled to ponder on the relationship of these two regions of thought."[21]

Indeed, Einstein observed that "the most unintelligible thing on the subject of the world is that it is intelligible."[22] And yet there is a rich and varied tradition of pursuing that intelligibility. A whole philosophical tradition stemming from Plato (the *Timaeus*), and Aristotle (his *Physics* and *Metaphysics*), and their medieval commentators, Christian, Jewish, and Muslim, would admit a wide range of complex distinctions between knowing God by reason and assenting to the divine mysteries in faith. Such a brand of hardy intellectualism exhibits numerous efforts to demonstrate the existence of God from the fact, structure, and movement of the world of experience. In that tradition, every created being exhibits a "vestige" of the divine.[23]

The very fact that so much of the cosmos is found to be so profoundly intelligible and so elegantly beautiful, luminous with that *splendor entis*—that "radiance of being" of which Aquinas speaks—invites the mind into its ultimate adventure: an exploration of the original mystery of it all. But there is a gently insistent question: "If they had the power to know so much...how did they fail to find sooner the Lord of these things?" Judith Wright, from her experience of world of nature, points us forward:

> My search is further.
> There's still to name and know
> beyond the flowers I gather,
> the one that does not wither—
> the truth from which they grow.[24]

These lines evoke a beautiful expression of medieval wisdom: "Creatures, as far as in them lies, do not turn us away from God but lead to God. If they do turn us away...that is due to those who, through their own fault, use them in ways that are contrary to reason."[25]

Some Medieval Pointers

Let us now sample the classic medieval account of the meaning of creation. In many ways, it is a surprising resource. In *Summa contra Gentiles*,[26] Aquinas asks whether the consideration of creatures is useful for the enlightenment of faith. His third reason is most fully expressed:

> The consideration of creation sparks in the human soul a love for the divine goodness. Whatever goodness and perfection is spread out in different creatures, it is a totality brought wholly together in the One who is in the source of all goodness....If therefore the goodness, the beauty and the delicacy [literally, *suavitas*] of creatures so lures the human soul, the source-good of God himself, diligently compared to the streams of goodness in the variety of creatures, inflames and attracts totally to itself our human souls.

As we intelligently explore the world of creation, we find that no creature is independent in its existence—a "stand-alone" explanation of itself—and that no element of our world is "the first cause" of everything. We need to learn to value the variety of created realities within the englobing mystery of existence, and receive it as a gift. According to this medieval vision, the variety of creation radiates from the one inexhaustible divine origin:

> For what exists in the cause in utter simplicity, is realised in the effect in a composite and pluriform manner....It is fitting, then, that there be a multiplicity and variety in created things so that God's image be found in them perfectly in accord with their mode of being.[27]

And yet there is a further point, too often overlooked. The mystery of creation, in its variety and unity, not only shares in the beauty and goodness of the Creator. The universe is brought into existence by an act of free creative love. Aquinas builds up to this conclusion in the following passage:

> God loves everything that exists....The will of God is the cause of everything; and so it follows that in so far as anything exists or is good under any aspect, it is willed by God. To whatever exists, God wills some good. So,

since love means nothing but wishing good to something or someone, it is clear that God loves everything that exists. But not in the same way as we human beings do. Because our will is not the cause of the goodness of things, but rather is moved by such good as an object of desire, so our love, by which we wish good for another, is not the cause of the good of that person. But rather, such goodness, real or imagined, provokes the love by which we will the good already possessed to be maintained, or a good to be added that is not already possessed. We work to that end. *But the love of God is infusing and creating the good in everything.*[28]

The being and variety of creation is total gift. God's love is not first attracted toward something already existing. Rather, everything, inasmuch as it exists, is loved into existence by the divine freedom: *amor Dei infundens et creans bonitatem in rebus.* Creation, from this point of view, is enacted as a communication of the divine joy in the existence of what is other. It is sheer gift: the (ultimate) Good is diffusive of itself (*Bonum est diffusivum sui*). The universe, therefore, is a divinely chosen order of being, and not a necessary emanation from, or completion of, a remote deity. In all its variety and connectedness, and, we might add, in its evolutionary potential, the created universe is a communication from the heart of God.

The stable world of specific natures linked in a great chain of being, as envisaged in the great medieval vision, differs from the evolutionary sense of the universe of today. In contemporary thinking, the whole is a process before it is an ordered collection of particular natures. But here, two remarks might be made. First, Aquinas exhibits a serene delight in the specific value of each element of creation as it has been divinely loved into being. Each being serves to manifest the divine goodness in a specific way. To that degree, such a view mitigates the cosmic sadness of an uncritical evolutionary myth. In its sense of the past, such a myth reads like an obituary for the casualties of evolution. The fittest survived; the weakest did not; and even what survives is subjected to the blind, harsh law that values only the future. In contrast, the medieval vision, even while it leaves unknown the mysterious ways of providence, finds an existential value in things simply because they exist—or once existed in a certain way at a certain time. It is a reminder to those who would hurry to frame the laws of evolution to consider two ideas. First, each individual entity is a world of mystery in the sheer fact of its existence. Before it can be considered a link in the chain of evolution, or as an aspect of the larger emerging complexity, it is, or was, *there*! The evolutionary potential—or lack of it—of the *Marella splendens*, or of any of eighty thousand extraordinarily complex creatures unearthed in the Burgess Shale in Western Canada, does not evacuate the fundamental wonder of its existence in the play and contingency of what happened in time.[29] The unique existence of the individual entity is so often "the missing link" in evolutionary thought.

Second, the seemingly purposeless variety of what once existed or is existing in its unique manner should make us wary of any premature closure on the story of what is going on. The human mind is not a detached spectator, but is part of the emerging process. Our reconstructions and extrapolations, whatever the progress of science, access only fragments of the meaning of the entire process. The Thomistic emphasis on the necessary plurality of creation and on the value of each existent not only contests the simplicity of evolutionary myths, but serves to keep evolutionary theory attentive to a truly inclusive wholeness. The system must remain open. The full story awaits, in patience and tentative exploration, the full understanding of creation that resides only in God.

While so much has changed as knowledge has expanded, it is worth noting that in the biblical vision of creation, other and higher forms of life were presumed. Their presence is now largely mediated to us only in the various liturgical prefaces in which the eucharistic assembly is invited to join with "angels and archangels, cherubim and seraphim" in a cosmic hymn of praise. At least, to evoke that largely forgotten biblical dimension of the cosmos suggests a more wonderful view of the living universe than that of the flat materialist anthropocentrism. The cosmic feelings and symbols of solidarity with all that is both below and above our form of life cannot but promote a greater awe and fresh questioning in the presence of so much that is still unknown. While the realm of created suprahuman intelligence is largely ignored in current preoccupations, it still has a suggestive power. It functions as a symbol, to say the very least, of dimensions of reality that have yet to be considered in our efforts to understand the commonwealth of life and the community of consciousness in the universe of our present perceptions.

The classical way of affirming the reality of creation led to a contemplative disclosure of the necessary existence of the Creator. That comparatively simple way of philosophical contemplation yields today to controlled experiment and brilliant mathematical hypotheses. The enormous intricacy of the "how" of the emergent process of the physical world seeks intelligibility in "theories of everything." These are elaborated as all-embracing mathematical schemes amalgamating all the fundamental forces and particles of physics together with the structure of space and time. Compared to such, the philosophical tradition looks vague and amateurish—until one realizes that many scientists are themselves loath to allow any specific science to pretend to swallow the mystery of the universe whole. Others opt for a universe of mere facticity: it simply happens to be what it is; and that is that. No deeper explanation is required. To appeal to an ultimate, let alone divine principle of explanation, looks suspiciously like another version of the "god of the gaps." It is crucial, then, to return to the point: God is not the missing factor in a mathematical or physical account of the way things are, but the all-pervasive mystery inherent in our best knowing, the Light in which the universe is luminous to itself in the human mind. As Herbert McCabe perceptively observes, past efforts to prove the existence of God were an implicit affirmation of the validity of scientific research.[30] There are interesting parallels in the experience of art.[31] The God question is a way of insisting that there can never be a finished explanation of everything. We exist, as it were, in an open system, opening into a limitless expanse of mystery from within our exploring intelligence. The human mind can never get to some intellectual place beyond the universe. Our explorations, be they intellectual, moral, or artistic, remain within it, to converge in separate ways on the original and ultimate question, posed in the relativity, the provisionality, and the dynamics of our knowing. The excess of implied meaning of all meaning, and the drive toward the sufficient reason of all our relative sufficient reasons, preclude any scientific or philosophical totalitarianism.

With this dark affirmation of God born out of the radical questionability of the world, we don't end up knowing more about the universe, except in recognizing its emergence from an incomprehensible fullness of Be-ing, life, and goodness.[32] God does not exist within the world as a part, or aspect, of what is. The universe exists in the boundless ocean of divine communicative Be-ing. The universe, in owing its being to the divine "Be-ing itself," participates in it, and thus stands forth from nothingness. Hence, to say that the cosmos or nature is God's creation is to set all our actual and potential experience of the world in a field of mystery, of supermeaning, and gift. The doctrine of creation makes space for the presence of the Creator as an all-embracing, all-originating mystery. God is no intraworldly system or function. Nor is the limitless Being of God a specific instance of some generic form of reality.[33] Rather, the reality of creation can be what it is, with its own laws, processes, and independent being. When there is no confusion of the Creator with creation, creation is given to us to explore, while the mind and heart that do the exploring are themselves dimensions of that one creation.

God, from this point of view, is "Be-ing that lets beings be."[34] God is more intimately present to each existent reality than it is to itself. Aquinas explains,

> God is present in all things, but not as part of their nature, nor as a modification of their being, but in the way something which acts is in contact with what it acts upon....Since God is by nature sheer Be-ing, it must be he who causes be-ing in creatures as his characteristic effect....God has this effect on created realities not only when they first begin to be, but as long as they are kept in being, as light is caused in the air by the sun as long as the air remains illuminated. So, for as long as anything is, God must be present to it in the way that it has being. But "to-be" [esse] is that which is the most intimate to each thing, and what most profoundly inheres in all things: everything else about any reality is potential compared to "to be." So God must be in everything, and in the most interior way.[35]

76

We can extend the meaning of creaturely being by understanding it as a process of becoming as the Creator continues not only to hold creation in being, but draws it on to its destined goal. In the words of Denis Edwards,

> Theology affirms that what enables the creature to be what it is, and enables it to become more than it is in itself, is the power of active self-transcendence, which is the pressure of the divine being acting upon creation from within....Evolutionary change is empowered by the dynamic presence of the absolute being of God. Evolutionary change occurs because of the presence of transforming love, which continually draws creation to a surprising and radically new future from within.[36]

Such a statement owes much to the evolutionary perspective of Karl Rahner. Though it might seem foreign to the classical medieval tradition, it can be understood, not so much opposed to the classic tradition, but as completing it. We need not pretend that the Scholastics had any familiarity with the contemporary evolutionary model of reality. Still, there is a precious insight in Thomist thinking: created autonomy does not set the creature against the Creator, but is a deeper manifestation of the creative presence of God. The more autonomous and self-transcendent a created reality, the more the intimate presence of the Creator to it. In other words, the Creator truly gives being, and the completion of that gift is its power to act. If our modern evolutionary optic understands a self-transcending surplus or excess in the emergent process of the world, this does not diminish the creative presence of God, but manifests it more fully. As Aquinas notes, "To detract from the perfection of the creature is to detract from the perfection of the divine power."[37]

An atheistic denial is seldom a rejection of God in the terms we have been employing here. The special antipathy that the nonbeliever feels toward "theists" is often in reaction to premature and often naïve religious or philosophical descriptions of God. If these suggest a smug religious answer suppressing intelligent questioning, the antipathy is intensified. When the devout mind naïvely proclaims God simply as a big (male) person, or as a disappointed manager of human affairs, or as the cosmic architect, or as the clockmaker who has slightly overwound his artefacts, or as the superforce in the cosmic process, things are a little too simple.

In the current evolutionary context, how, then, should we think of God? An eminent American philosopher instructively remarks,

> To speculate creatively and imaginatively as to what the "personality" or "character" must be like that of a Creator in whose image this astonishing universe of ours is made, with its prodigal abundance of energy, its mind-boggling complexity yet simplicity, its fecundity of creative spontaneity, its ever-surprising fluid inter-weaving of order and chance, law and apparent chaos, and so forth. Must not the personality of such a Cre-ator be charged not only with unfathomable wisdom, power and exuberant generosity, but also with dazzling "imaginative" creativity—might we say a daring Cosmic Gambler who delights in working out his providence by a creative synthesis of both law and order, on the one hand, and chance, risk, spontaneity, on the other—a "coincidence of opposites" as St. Bonaventure put it long ago?[38]

How might a more realistic and reverent dialogue between rep-resentatives of different disciplines be conducted in the interests of an integral ecology? The following words are something of a Christian protocol for entering and promoting dialogue between science and religion:

> We need each other to be what we must be. Science can purify religion from error and superstition; religion can purify science from idolatry and false absolutes. Each can draw the other into a wider world, a world in which both can flourish…the vitality and significance of theol-ogy for humanity will in a profound way be reflected in its ability to incorporate these findings.…The matter is urgent. Contemporary developments in science chal-lenge theology far more deeply than did the introduc-tion of Aristotle into Western Europe in the thirteenth

century....Christians will inevitably assimilate the prevailing ideas about the world, and today these are deeply shaped by science. The only question is whether they will do this critically or unreflectively, with depth and nuance or with a shallowness that debases the Gospel and leaves us ashamed before history.[39]

By daring to explore agreements and divergences, a theology of creation and a comprehensive philosophy of science may well take a huge step in clarifying the emergent properties and evolutionary dynamics of our world for the development of a truly integral ecology.

The human spirit brings another dimension into the universe—the universe, conscious of itself, exploring itself in the human mind, and, for that matter, celebrating itself in the human heart and imagination, so that, as Goethe would say, the human is the first conversation that nature holds with God, its Creator. Philosophical and theological questions take us to the limits. Regardless of how we account for the wonder and complexity of the universe and for the emergence of life on planet Earth, the way forward is to conceive of the Creator's causality as transcending all modes of finite causation in the activity of creating and sustaining the universe. The activity of the Creator respects the seemingly chaotic randomness of the entire process, yet providentially works in its every detail to achieve an end evident only to the Creator, "the Lord and Giver of Life," in the words of the Nicene Creed.

CONCLUSION

In the meantime, faith, hope, and love continue to search. The horizon of Christian theology is determined by the love of God incarnate in Christ, crucified and risen, and by the Spirit laboring through the whole groaning universe (see Rom 8) to lead us to life eternal. Theology never ends its search, especially when faced with cosmic and evolutionary questions. These questions not only challenge faith to give an account of itself, but to learn, from whatever source, something more of how God acts and what kind of God is involved.

This chapter has treated the realities of the Creator, creation, and ecology from the perspective of human consciousness, the better to interiorize our sense of the presence of God and to extend the possibility of dialogue on many fronts. Such an approach moves "from the inside out," so to speak, with the emphasis on experience, the phenomenon of consciousness and intentionality. This contrasts with a "from the outside in" perspective, with its concern for the purely objective, but without an explicit focus on the interiority of the subject. Modern science has demonstrated a magnificence in its concentration on empirical data regarding the material constitution of the universe and the stages of evolution. It has, however, tended to neglect another kind of data, namely, the data of consciousness that enable human consciousness, science, ecology, and the life of the spirit to be examined in a more ample and open-minded fashion—in the interests of an integral ecology. I hope, therefore, to have intensified the ecological sense of dwelling in creation and dwelling in God.

CHAPTER 5

Christ and Integral Ecology

F OR CHRISTIAN FAITH, the incarnation is a singular, constitutive event: "for in him the whole fullness of deity [*theotes*] dwells bodily [*somatikos*]" (Col 2:9; see John 1:14).[1] The event of the incarnation includes and expands through the resurrection and ascension of Christ. For life on earth and the ecology of this planet, faith must continue to ponder the significance of the Word made flesh. Under the following three headings we present the incarnation as an expanding event with consequences for the understanding of ecology:

1. The Incarnation as an Expanding Event;
2. The Fulfillment of Nature; and
3. Existence Transformed.

THE INCARNATION AS AN EXPANDING EVENT

First, Christ's resurrection and ascension do not mean that he becomes disincarnate or disembodied. Rather, he is fully embodied in the world as it will be.[2] Compared to his transformed embodiment, we human beings are not yet fully embodied as we are destined to be. In other words, only in the light of Christ's resurrection and ascension can the incarnation be fully understood.

Unless backlit by such a radiance, there would be no story to tell and none worth the telling; and there would be no one in any age disposed to listen to it. If Jesus had remained under the conditions of his terrestrial existence, if he had not ascended to the realm of God's new creation, there would be no capacity to receive the fullness of grace, nor any inkling of life transformed—and already in the process of being drawn into the divine realm (Col 3:3). A terrestrial and ecological perspective emerges in that Jesus has received the name that is above every name, so that all creation might confess him as Lord to the glory of the Father (Phil 2:9–11).

The Relational Body

The relational scope of the expanding incarnation can be blocked by the narrowly empiricist attitude that reduces the body to something I "have," and that is exclusively *mine*. In that case, "my body" would be understood as one among innumerable physical bodies. It would be imagined as disconnected from the network of relationships shaping human consciousness and unaffected by the ecology of this earthly biosphere. The consideration, therefore, of *somebody* detached from personal consciousness and unaffected by the ecological relationships essential to life on this planet inevitably constricts an understanding of human beings in their fully relational earthly coexistence. Consequently, there is something fundamentally awry when theology treats the embodied reality of the incarnate Word in this jejune fashion.

In contrast to the depersonalized objectification of the individual body, a far richer and more realistic approach opens when the bodily reality is appreciated as the "saturated phenomenon" of a personal *somebody*. It connotes a special sense of immediacy and unobjectifiable intimacy regarding oneself, others, and all living things that make up the great communion of life on this planet. "My body" is not merely something I possess, but is rather the field of communication with all others. The body, therefore, intimately constitutes the person's being in the world. It implies possibilities of intimate self-giving and self-disclosure—as in the case of erotic or maternal love. In this sense, the flesh of our embodied consciousness is a field of mutual indwelling, and of being with and for the other. It reaches a special intensity in the *eros* and generativity of love, as one's bodily being is reexperienced through the flesh of the other, and in the all-nurturing beauty of nature.[3]

One's body, then, is more than its objectification as one physical body in a material world of many similar objects. Rather, the body is constituted as a field of conscious interactions, a zone of incarnated relationships.[4] For the body of my conscious being is affected by the encompassing phenomenon of the world, and, in turn, affects it. It is at once an elemental bonding with the world, an immediate exposure to it, an immediate participation in it, and a primal communication within it.[5] Through such bodily experience, the human person participates in the world of time and space, and becomes familiar with the creativity, dynamism, and final limits of nature itself. The body, with its senses, consciousness, and imagination, is our immediate interactive immersion in the communion of life on this planet.

Such an understating of body as incorporation in the communion of life on this planet, and within the vibrant network of relationships in which one exists in the world, can serve as an analogy for the expanding event of the incarnation. The flesh of the Word incarnate is a matrix of manifold and interrelated dimensions of embodiment. It exists grounded in relationships to other human beings, to all living things, to the earth, to the land, time, space, and nature. The body language of the New Testament extends to differing kinds of corporeal relationships—the sexual, maternal, familial, social, ecological, cosmic, to throw light on the expanding reality of the Body of Christ (Eph 4:4).

The Body of Christ

The incarnate Word is still *somebody*. Christ, crucified, risen, and ascended to the right hand of the Father, is not beyond embodied communication with the world—as it occurs in the Eucharist, the primary example. Christian consciousness is primarily receptive to the self-giving bodily reality of Christ. There is no bypassing the communicative reality of his "flesh" (1 John 4:2). The "flesh" of Jesus, when transformed itself, will be transformative in its effect: "the bread that I will give for the life of the world is my flesh" (John 6:51). From the Johannine perspective, the flesh of Christ is a field of mutual indwelling (see John 6:56). In the teeth of objections to this confronting realism (v. 52), Jesus makes his provocation even more intense:

> Very truly, I tell you, unless you eat the flesh of the Son of Man and drink his blood, you have no life in you. Those who eat my flesh and drink my blood have eternal life, and I will raise them up on the last day; for my flesh is true food and my blood is true drink. Those who eat my flesh and drink my blood abide in me, and I in them. (John 6:53–56)

For Paul, on the other hand, the Body of Christ is the sphere of the new creation. It implies something more than a sociological metaphor, for it looks to an incorporation of his "members" into the transformed Body of Christ. Paul pushes Christian consciousness toward a distinctive realism. Regardless of how this might be articulated, it goes further than any facile metaphorical application. The apostle presents the Christian community as composed of members of the Body of Christ: "For just as the body is one and has many members, and all the members of the body, though many, are one body, so it is with Christ" (1 Cor 12:12). With the plurality and diversity of the many spiritual gifts, "you are the body of Christ and individually members of it" (1 Cor 12:27). Between Christ and his members, there is indeed a corporeal relationship, but this in the sphere of the Spirit: "But anyone united to the Lord becomes one spirit with him" (1 Cor 6:17), so that body is now a "temple of the Holy Spirit" (v. 19). The injunction follows: "glorify God in your body" (v. 20b). It accords with Paul's injunction to glorify God in every aspect of our bodily being, even that of our ecological embodiment in the life of this planet.

The provocative force of Paul's remarks implies a distinctive realism. Christians must live their Christ-embodied reality, not in some celestial sphere, but in the here-and-now world of erotic impulses and allure: there is no "mystical body" on that level! The body, however, remains the realm of communication with the risen Lord through the power of his Spirit. Indeed, this Spirit exercises a corporate influence, to be, as it were, the shared breath, the living atmosphere, the vital principle of the Body of Christ, manifested in the profusion of gifts. In this one Spirit, "we were all baptized into one body...and we were all made to drink of one Spirit" (1 Cor 12:13). Thus, the Spirit is by no means a disembodied reality, but rather the sustaining principle of the Body. This corporeal reality is progressively understood through physical analogies related to movement, energy, joining, and drinking. The Spirit invigorates the Body of Christ as the vital breath; and the Church, as Christ's Body, breathes by the life-giving air of the Spirit.

Both the manifold Pauline senses of the "body of Christ" and the reality of the life-giving "flesh" of Christ typical of a more Johannine approach converge as dimensions of a distinctive Christian realism. The resurrection and ascension of Jesus do not mean that he has ceased to be God's bodily organ of communication. Rather, the incarnational event expands, and in a manner proper to the new creation inaugurated at Easter.

The transformed Body of Christ presumes a new mode of corporeality, with its own distinctive mode of knowing and sensibility.[6] Mind and heart are affected by personal participation in the vertical and horizontal expansion of the incarnation. The scale includes the vertical, since it arises only from the gift of God, from "on high," unconditioned by any human condition. But horizontal also, since there is room for formulating knowledge, educating sensibilities, and shaping commitments within the experience of the Church in history, especially as it breathes the air of this planet today.

THE FULFILLMENT OF NATURE

Christ's bodily transformation must include nature itself in that new creation when "death will be no more" (Rev 21:4), and when life is ultimately fulfilled in the face-to-face vision of God. In Christ, a new cosmic and theocentric order comes into being. Its field of generative relationships constitutes a new nature, a new principle of action, anticipated in the Church's celebration of the Eucharist. In the ascended Jesus, time, space, body, and nature are refashioned. History, instead of being a concatenation of episodic events, is caught up in the updraft of all things being gathered into Christ.

Thus, Christ's Body is the organic field of his relationship to the world. It affects, and, in turn, is affected by the manifold reality of our embodied coexistence in him. Though Christ is the form, goal, and agent of a transformed existence, his risen body continues in its "natal bond" with the world of his incarnation. His relationship with the world expresses the immediacy of his exposure to the world, precisely in the process of its transformation in him. Paul goes so far as to say that in his flesh he is "completing what is lacking in Christ's afflictions for the sake of his body, that is, the church" (Col 1:24). Through their incorporation into the Body of Christ, the members of his Body awaken to the world on its way to transformation. Such is the distinctive realism of Christian corporate existence. It discloses a distinctive sense of intersubjectivity and mutual indwelling within the field of incarnate communication. Jesus prays "that they may all be one. As you, Father, are in me, and I am in you, may they also be in us" (John 17:21).[7] The incarnate "word of life" (1 John 1:1) takes the form of a communal existence. This is declared with the vigor of an immediately sensuous and affect-charged experience of hearing, seeing, touching, and union:

> What was from the beginning, what we have heard, what we have seen with our eyes, what we have looked at and touched with our hands, concerning the word of life—this life was revealed, and we have seen it and testify to it, and declare to you the eternal life that was with the Father and was revealed to us—we declare to you what we have seen and heard. (1 John 1:1–3)

The realism of the incarnation is eschatological. It finds expression most concretely in Christ's promise to return in glory at the end of time, as in the words of Jesus in John's Gospel:

> In my Father's house there are many dwelling places. If it were not so, would I have told you that I go to prepare a place for you? And if I go and prepare a place for you, I will come again and take you to myself, so that where I am, there you may be also. (John 14:2–3)

The number and character of these "dwelling places" remains a fascinating question. Faith must move beyond itself in hope and in the longing of love if Christians are to be released into the fullest dimensions of receptivity to the gift of God. The "theological virtues" need to be properly *theological*, and therefore attuned to the incalculable action of the Spirit, to the inexpressible mystery of the Father, and to the transformation of earthly humanity that has occurred in the risen and ascended Christ. Otherwise, the life of faith could become fixated on "seeing" and holding onto Jesus in his previous mode of accessibility (see John 20:17). Such an attitude would fail to recognize the universal and enduring scope of what God was bringing about in Christ and the Spirit.

Furthermore, the inclusion of the suffering body of our humanity and of the earth itself is suggested in John's depiction of the risen body of the Lord still marked by the wounds of the cross (John 20:24–26; see Rev 5:6–9). The Risen One is ever the Crucified One, still in compassionate solidarity with suffering humanity and with the whole "groaning" reality of creation (see Rom 8:18–25). The transformation of Christ's humanity beyond death does not imply "excarnation," but a new form of incarnation. A bodily "mutation" has occurred: "the bread that I will give for the life of the world is my flesh" (John 6:51). By sacramentally assimilating Christ's flesh and blood, given and outpoured for the life of the world, believers are conformed to his risen life: "Those who eat my flesh and drink my blood have eternal life, and I will raise them up on the last day; for my flesh is true food and my blood is true drink" (John 6:54–55).

Communion and Indwelling

In short, Christ's risen existence continues and expands his communication in the flesh. Embodied in this way, he is the focus and source of a new order of relationships for which no metaphor is adequate. The limits of mutual indwelling inherent in the physicality of being a mere body are now transformed into a new mode of mutual coinherence: "Those who eat my flesh and drink my blood abide in me, and I in them" (John 6:56; see 15:4, 6). In this eschatological realm, believers "abide in the Son and in the Father" (1 John 2:24; see 3:24). They begin to inhabit a field of love in which earthly *eros* is subsumed into the *agape* of the divine self-giving: "God is love, and those who abide in love abide in God, and God abides in them" (1 John 4:16).

To the degree faith assimilates Christ's flesh and blood and Spirit, there is new sight, hearing, touching, tasting, eating and drinking, feeling, and indwelling—the new senses of faith, as Origen recognized so clearly.[8] Because of its unobjectifiable immediacy and mutuality, the Body of Christ is the field of an intersubjectivity that "earths" and enfleshes faith's experience of the Risen One. Neither a spiritual immateriality nor a sensate materialism is implied, but rather a participation in genuinely bodily life in the world affected by the transformation that has occurred. To a contemplative faith, there is a certain sacramentality to be affirmed in the world of nature itself—nature as a gift, never apart from grace, nature under the promise of all things made new.

EXISTENCE TRANSFORMED

Because Christian imagination cannot rest content with a play of metaphors, it continually seeks to serve the all-inclusive, corporate reality of Christ: "for you have died, and your life is hidden with Christ in God. When Christ who is your life is revealed, then you also will be revealed with him in glory" (Col 3:3–4).

A New Self in Christ

A newly embodied self emerges: "you have stripped off the old self with its practices and clothed yourself with the new self, which is being renewed in knowledge according to the image of its creator" (Col 3:9–10). In this renewed embodied existence, believers are offered a new sense of corporate coexistence: "In that renewal there is no longer Greek and Jew, circumcised and uncircumcised, barbarian, Scythian, slave and free, but Christ is all and in all" (Col 3:11).

The great saint of East and West, Maximus the Confessor, speaks of the human being as "the laboratory in which everything is concentrated and itself naturally mediates between the extremities of each division, having been drawn into everything in a good and fitting way through its development."[9] More recently, under the influence of modern cosmology, Teilhard de Chardin perceptively remarked,

> My own body is not these or those cells which belong exclusively to me. It is what, in these cells and in the rest of the world, feels my influence and reacts against me. *My* matter is not a *part* of the universe that I possess *totaliter*. It is the totality of the universe that I possess *partialiter*.[10]

With his pan-christic perspective, Teilhard insists, "Christ must be kept as large as creation and remains its Head. No matter how large we discover the world to be, the figure of Jesus, risen from the dead, must embrace it in its entirety,"[11] and make room for its concrete particularity.

In the totality and particularity, the risen and ascended Christ suggests both a movement and a horizon, as in the words of Jesus, "I go to prepare a place for you" (John 14:2) in the Father's house of many rooms. He goes on to assure his disciples, "And if I go and prepare a place for you, I will come again and take you to myself, so that where I am, there you may be also" (John 14:3).[12] The ascension, therefore, is not a mythological addition to the incarnation and resurrection, but the movement and horizon in which God's comprehensive, transformative action is occurring. From that point of view, Christ's ascension and departure from this world amounts to bringing the Christian heaven into existence. For Jesus ascends, not simply in his individual humanity, but as embodying a world, perfected, transformed, and offered to the Father, and diaphanous with the Light (Rev 21:23). According to the explicit promise of Jesus to Nathanael—as the representative of all future disciples—"You will see heaven opened and the angels of God ascending and descending upon the Son of Man" (John 1:51). The hitherto "closed heaven" is now opened in such a way that the glorified Son of Man is the new channel of communication between God and creation. Jesus will be the new Jacob's ladder (Gen 28:12–17), connecting what is above with what is below, what is at the center and what is at the circumference of existence (see John 3:13). Jesus, risen and ascended, is therefore the realization of a new communication between God and the world. He who is most intimate to the Father became accessible in the flesh of this world, so that believers can now find their way to the Father, and a dwelling in his house (John 14:1–4).[13] The ascended Christ is constituted, in the full relationality of his existence, as "being for" the world. Ever active in his eucharistic self-giving, and breathing forth his Spirit, he anticipates the "sublime communion" for which all creation is destined.[14]

Time in Christ

Yet here, the most complex questions arise. The compact paschal event of Jesus's death, burial, resurrection, and glorification unfolds over the course of time; and is revealed in time.[15] There are implications for understanding the new creation as "time in Christ" as it is being lived and understood. When the crucified One has been raised up, it is the beginning of the new creation. The old world of time and space is not left undisturbed. In this new creation, Jesus does not become disembodied or disincarnate, as we have been stressing. Consequently, he is not rendered timelessly static. It is not as though nothing more happens for him; or, at the other extreme, that time has no goal and dissipates meaninglessly in an endless flow of discrete moments. Rather, the ascended Jesus inaugurates "the fullness of time." In what and who he is, he brings time to its fullness, gathering the scattered moments of undecided time into a flow directed to the glory of the Father. Within this new time, the Body of Christ grows toward that ultimate point when God will be "all in all" (1 Cor 15:28).

Regarding the Body of Christ, we are justified in speaking of a *process* of glorification. That does not mean, however, that each moment of the process has no value in itself, or that, in part or in whole, it is producing the glory of Jesus. Christ is not in time as subject to it, but rather, the whole flow of time is subject to him: "Jesus Christ is the same yesterday and today and forever" (Heb 13:8). Indeed, the incarnation as it expands in the resurrection-ascension initiates a new form of temporality. Christ has time and makes space for his followers in a new way.[16] Von Balthasar suggests that the time of the forty days prefigures the time of the Church in which Christ is encountered in the sacraments and in other ways.[17] Nevertheless, Christ's ascension signifies the end of a previous mode of life. He has vanished from the visibilities of earthly existence. That resultant invisibility makes clear that the Church does not possess, control, or contain Christ. Rather, the totality of all creation is contained by him. Christ is not "in" the sacraments, just as he is not "in" the world. Rather, elements of the world—the bread and wine, oil, water, and so on—are, through the action of the Spirit, assumed "into Christ," transfigured by him as anticipations of the new creation—to become the sacraments of faith. The time of the sacraments has no end while history continues.

Fullness of Time

In short, Christ is the fullness of time. He is not subject to its fragmentation but freely gathers what was, what is, and what is to come into this incarnate being. In the light of the ever-expanding event of the incarnation, history and all creation takes on an eschatological density. Through the ascension, Christ rises above history, but not in flight from it. Rather, that history has a new density and direction. Under the guidance of the Spirit, it is made to serve the fullness of our embodied coexistence in Christ, as the incarnation event expands from one generation to the next to include all that is good in creation. Time no longer has the power to delay the realization of our true selves in him, nor is it allowed to fragment and undermine our deepest relationship to the world. And yet, the time of Christ is the time of eschatological surprises. It is not simply biological time (with its aging and entropy), but the time of an ever broader and deeper realization of our true selves in the Body of Christ. From this point of view, time in Christ has entered the trinitarian eternity of loving exchange. Its flow and direction remain so that the interpersonal communion existing between the Father and the Son can be extended to all ages, from one generation to the next (see John 17:20–24), and into the life of the world to come.

Therefore, the ascension does not take Christ out of time, but is the condition for his complete immersion in it, as its fullness. Faith is the consciousness of having time "in him," so that he, "the firstborn of all creation" and "the firstborn from the dead" (Col 1:15–18), becomes the measure and goal of time. If time in classical parlance is "the measure of motion," the Body of Christ is the fullest measure of what is truly moving in history and in the universe itself—gifts are poured out "for [the] building up of the body of Christ, until all of us come to the unity of the faith and of the knowledge of the Son of God, to maturity, to the measure of the full stature of Christ" (Eph 4:12–13). Jesus, in his ascent to the Father, brings time of the world to its redemptive completion.

In this era of time after the ascension, though faith believes without seeing, Christ is more perfectly present in each "now," and in each aspect of the world, than could ever have been the case in his earthly life. The ascension is the point from which Luke, for example, looks back over the whole life and mission of Jesus; and from which he looks forward into the unbounded mission of the Church. The retrospective view entails the recognition of Christ as the individual Jesus of Nazareth. The prospective view recognizes the living, present reality of the crucified and risen Jesus as the Christ—and the fulfillment that is promised. More precisely, the history of Christian consciousness contains a recollection of both postresurrection appearances of Jesus, and their ending (1 Cor 15:3–11). But this ending leads us into the time of his ascension in which Jesus lives as the conqueror of death, and as embodying the new creation that will be fully realized with his return at the end of history.

Consequently, faith is earthed in the reality of an ending, a departure, a closure—and a subsequent expansion—in the time of faith and in the light of the Spirit. Yet Christ ascends into the indefinability of the realm of God from which the Spirit, the other Paraclete, will come (John 16:7).[18] In the actual free dispensation of God's grace and mercy, the objective offer of the gift of God— the incarnation in all its mysteries—must be accompanied by the God-given capacity to receive it, namely, the gift of the Spirit (see John 16:23).

The World in Christ

After these few remarks on the time of the ascension, the related question of "where" arises. That is easier to ask than to answer. Has the body of Christ been relocated in some other realm? Admittedly, metaphors of location cannot be avoided (e.g., John

14:3). However, that does not necessitate the invention of a sacred space or heavenly location somehow added to the physical world of our experience. Nor does it mean the invention of some form of celestial physics. But there is a more destructive extreme when the ascension is taken to mean, in effect, the displacement of the physical reality of Christ—what amounts to an "excarnation." If the Word was made flesh (John 1:14), does the present situation of Christ, ascended into heaven, suggest that his flesh, the bodily being of his earthly life, has been volatilized and so spiritualized that the incarnation ceases to be after his resurrection and ascension? The only possible solution is to be found in a more comprehensive theology of the incarnation so that it includes the resurrection and ascension—and indeed, the formation of the Body of Christ through time and space. Christ, at each phase of the incarnation, remains the same person (Luke 24:39; Heb 13:8), even if the incarnation is an expanding event, as Christ draws to himself all creation.[19] In the great "cosmic" christological statements of John and Paul (John 1:3–5; 1 Cor 15:25–28; Eph 1:3–10; Col 1:15–17; Heb 1:1–4; Rev 1:12–16), the overriding concern of the New Testament writers is not to locate Christ within the cosmos from which he has departed, but to view the totality of the world in its fabric and movement within the redemptive reality of Christ. He embodies the totality of the new creation, its origin, form, coherence, and goal.

The Return of Christ

With the ascension of Jesus into the cloud of divine glory, faith must enter its "cloud of unknowing"—in accord with mystical tradition of the *via negativa*. There will be an absence and the darkness born of the passing away of familiar knowledge with its fixed bearings and clear outlines. But out of this darkness, Christ will appear—the fulfillment of all our human searching and hoping. He will not come as an idea, but in his personal and bodily identity. He returns as the Word incarnate *in person* and in the full relationality of his identity as Son of the Father, our brother, in whom all things were made.

Jesus, risen and ascended, "deconstructs" the categories and language of mundane thinking and even that of religious expression.

The holding capacity of the old wineskins becomes inadequate considering the fresh wine of revelation (Matt 9:16–17; Mark 2:21–22; Luke 5:36–39). Christ has ascended beyond this world of creation into that of the new creation, the inexpressible realm in anticipation of God being "all in all" (1 Cor 15:28). The life of faith is now a time of waiting for the revelation and advent of this other realm when Christ returns. Human thinking may well look forward to that unimaginable event, and be tempted to fill the present with an array of definite objects of shape, color, and temporal sequence to describe what is to come in the language and imagery of the present provisional world. That temptation throws light on the strange paradox that occurs at the heart of revelation. For all the explicitness of the promise of eternal life, for all the variety of images employed to that purpose, the Scriptures, in fact, exhibit a marked reserve in describing the realities they most witness to—a new heaven and a new earth.

A triple silence in the Christian narrative can be detected. There is the dark silence of death, when the Word is silenced, and Jesus is dead and buried. And then, there is the luminous silence in which faith trembles before the empty tomb, and witnesses to the appearances of the risen One, to be faced with the utterly other and the utterly new. Then, this is followed by the further silence of the Son's ascension to the Father, into the heart of the Mystery that is the source of all gifts and giving. The singular parable of Christ's life, death, resurrection, and ascension takes none of the waiting or silence out of the hope it inspires. It must wait on what no eye has seen, what no ear has heard, and what no human heart has conceived regarding the fulfillment of God's promises (see 1 Cor 2:9). Though faith follows the ascended Christ into the universal reach of his presence, there is no assurance of clarity, and the ways of God remain beyond all human calculation (Rom 11:33). No matter how unreserved the promise of eternal life for those who believe, "what we will be has not yet been revealed" (1 John 3:2). All that we are told is known is that "when he is revealed, we will be like him," in the full evidence of the Light. His ascension precludes any attempt to fit the gift of God into the proportions of human calculation.

The humility of the early New Testament witnesses is evidenced in that they have left a sobering record of their naïvety. Though

Christ had "presented himself alive to them by many convincing proofs" (Acts 1:3), unable to get beyond their own narrow horizon, they had asked, "Lord, is this the time when you will restore the kingdom to Israel?" (Acts 1:6). Jesus's answer is instructive: "It is not for you to know the times or the periods that the Father has set by his own authority" (Acts 1:7). These disciples are then commissioned to be his witnesses—"in Jerusalem, in all Judea and Samaria, and to the ends of the earth" (Acts 1:8). And so, the restoration of the kingdom to Israel ceases to be their pressing concern. Even the oldest recorded prayer in the New Testament, "Maranatha! Our Lord, come!" (cf. 1 Cor 16:22; Rev 22:20), so expressive of longing and hope, presupposes nothing other than the identity of Jesus—crucified, risen, and ascended, and promising his return at the end of time. Hope certainly anticipates a new creation with a bodily sharing in the glory of Christ, when the perishable, the dishonorable, the weak, and the physical, will become, in conformity to him, imperishable, glorious, powerful, spiritual (1 Cor 15:42–44). Belief in the ascended Christ outstrips any imaginative ability to represent the future. Mind, heart, and imagination must yield to patience and hope in him who "by the power at work within us is able to accomplish abundantly far more than all we can ask or imagine" (Eph 3:20). The effect of the ascension is to discourage any attempt to reduce the future to the categories and structures of this present sphere of earthly experience: "hope that is seen is not hope" (Rom 8:24). Hope expands to its proper proportions only by following Christ in his ascent to the Father and awaiting his return. Even the best intentions of prayer remain subject to the inspiration of the Spirit: "for we do not know how to pray as we ought, but that very Spirit intercedes with sighs too deep for words" (Rom 8:26). Christian consciousness must learn to live, not only by not clinging to him in narrow patterns of understanding and representation of the world from which Jesus has ascended (John 20:17), but also cultivate an openness (cf. Acts 1:6–7; Rom 8:26–27). The mundane desires latent even in our best prayers and hopes must yield to the incalculable dimensions of the Spirit and will of the Father.

With all its symbolic retinue of metaphor and symbol, the ascension is the paradigmatic instance of the imagination of faith going beyond its powers of expression, even while relying on the mediation of images (ascent, the cloud, the Father's right hand, heavenly figures, and so forth).[20] Faith follows the ascended One to transcend the world of experience, to move beyond the available world of representations and conceptual systems, so to go into the unutterable reality of communion with him who now draws the faithful into the unity existing between himself and the Father.[21] Even though a new order of existence has been inaugurated, there is a distance, a hiddenness, and a radical demand inherent in it:

> Seek the things that are above, where Christ is, seated at the right hand of God. Set your minds on things that are above, not on things that are on earth, for you have died, and your life is hidden with Christ in God. When Christ who is your life is revealed, then you also will be revealed with him in glory. (Col 3:1–4)

As Bulgakov wisely remarks, the ascension, far from being a withdrawal or diminishment in terms of God's relationship to the world, shows forth the God-world relationship in a clearer light.[22] In the ascent of the glorified humanity of Christ, time and space are newly configured. The hypostatic relationship of the divine person to humanity is not lessened, but expanded. The continuance and expansion of the humanity of the ascended Christ now makes clear for faith that there is no God without the world; and no world apart from God. To use a spatial metaphor, the world, owned, claimed, finalized in Christ, is now forever "in God." The ascension is not completed in the exaltation of Christ alone, but spills over, as it were, into the eventual ascension of all.[23] To that degree, it has the character of an unbounded event of universal effect. Though all things are now subjected to him, he is exalted in his subjection to the Father so that "God may be all in all" (1 Cor 15:28). Although he now possesses "the name that is above every name" (Phil 2:9), and all creation exalts the name of Jesus, he exercises his universal lordship "to the glory of God the Father" (Phil 2:11).

For the believer, the mysteries of faith—above all, the light and atmosphere of a new creation—must be received on their own terms. Just as the risen Jesus entered the locked rooms to the surprise of his fearful disciples, the life of faith must remain

96

responsive to the light of Christ and the fresh air of his Spirit. The conclusion of John's Gospel remains a healthy reminder: the risen Jesus is not contained within the linear print of any book—or of all the books of the world (John 21:25). The phenomenon exceeds all efforts to express it.

Ascension and the Assumption of Mary

Here, questions about the ascension, the Body of Christ, and materiality of creation[24] suggest a reference to the Catholic doctrine of the assumption of Our Lady, solemnly defined in 1950. This is one more point where, theologically speaking, the intentionality of faith has hurried past its powers of expression. If Mary is declared to be assumed, body and soul, into heaven, then the corporate, historical authority of the Catholic Church is thereby committed to a view of materiality, corporeality, and physicality in a way that is largely beyond our powers of expression, in either conceptual or even imaginative terms. Here, we can do little more than note that it would be of great ecumenical and ecological significance if our understandings of the ascension of Christ and the assumption of Mary interacted more positively. In the concrete liturgical unfolding of Catholic tradition, the ascension of Jesus would be deprived of its salvific significance if it remained unrelated to the assumption of Mary as cause to effect. Conversely, the assumption, if more clearly connected to the ascension of Christ, would have a clearer ecclesiological and ecological significance.

Faith stretches forward and upward. Ambrose of Milan expressed the cosmic sweep of the mystery of Christ with the words, "In Christ's resurrection, the world arose. In Christ's resurrection, the heavens arose; in Christ's resurrection, the earth itself arose."[25] Accordingly, we have been emphasizing the significance of the ascension as the completion and expansion of incarnation, in the hope of glimpsing the connections between the incarnation, the ascension, and the universal transformation anticipated in the Catholic doctrine of Mary "assumed body and soul into heaven." In such a context, the assumption of Mary is a concrete symbol of the overbrimming significance of the ascension itself. Now assumed into the glory of Christ, she is the anticipation of the heaven of a transfigured creation.[26] In that regard, Mary is the paradigmatic instance of creation open to, collaborating with, and transformed by the creative mystery of God in Christ. As the Mother of Christ, she symbolizes the generativity of creation under the power of the Spirit. In her, as the Advent antiphon has it, "the earth has been opened to bud forth the Savior." In its confession of the assumption, Christian hope finds a specific confirmation. In Mary, now assumed body and soul into the heaven of God and Christ, our humanity, our world, and even our history, have reached their divinely destined term. She embodies the reality of our world as having received into itself the mystery that is to transform the universe in its entirety. The seer of the Apocalypse invites his readers to share the vision of "the holy city, the new Jerusalem, coming down out of heaven from God, prepared as a bride adorned for her husband" (Rev 21:2). Such a vision is the background for both a theology of the ascension of him who uniquely descended from on high, and for Mary's assumption as the New Eve and her place in the new creation. In Mary's assumption, our world becomes diaphanous to the glory of God, and the great cosmic marriage begins. The Spirit has brought forth in her the beauty of creation as God sees it. In her, human history has come to its maturity, its age of consent, to surrender to the transcendent love for which it was destined. Out of such a union, the whole Christ of a transfigured creation is born. Thus, while the focus of Christian hope is in Christ's death, resurrection, and ascension, there is a *reprise*, as it were, of the paschal mystery and its efficacy in the assumption of Mary into heaven; the gift of Christ's transforming grace has already been received and attained its transforming effect. The ascended Christ has conformed her to himself, so that she embodies receptivity to the gift of God—who has "raised us up with him and seated us with him in the heavenly places in Christ Jesus, so that in the ages to come he might show the immeasurable riches of his grace in kindness toward us in Christ Jesus" (Eph 2:6–7).

Assumed into the heaven of her Son's ascension, Mary is no more subject to the rule of death (1 Cor 15:42–58). Her transformed existence is no longer enclosed in physicality of a world undisturbed by the resurrection and the ascension of the crucified One. United to Christ, Mary lives and acts, and continues to act, as the Mother of the Church. In the heaven of Christ, her intercessory prayer and compassionate involvement has a measureless influence. Invoked as Mother of the Church, Our Lady Help of Christians, Mother of Mercy, Mother of Perpetual Help, Our Lady of Guadalupe, and so on (indeed, in all the invocations of the Litany of Loreto, and more), she is present in the divine realm of endless life and love. Mary of Nazareth is the name of a historical person—the Mother of Jesus. Yet history has no record of her life except through the documents of faith, above all, the Gospels of the New Testament. It is significant in the present context that she has become known to faith only through the immense transformation that took place in the resurrection and ascension of her Son, and its impact on human consciousness through faith, hope, and love. The assumption enables faith to glimpse the "opened heaven" of Jesus's promise to the disciples in his conversation with Nathanael: "Very truly, I tell you, you will see heaven opened and the angels of God ascending and descending upon the Son of Man" (John 1:51). Her Son embodies the open heaven of communication between God and creation. But in Mary, the effects of that communication are anticipated in ways appropriate to her vocation as Mother of the whole Christ, head and members; and, indeed, Mother of the earth redeemed.

In short, the salvific effect of the ascension of Christ enters the life of faith and the span of hope through the assumption of Mary—a determining feature of Catholic ecclesial experience and tradition. Not to mention it in the present context would leave the ascension of Christ without its most personal effect. Furthermore, if the assumption of Mary is left disconnected from the ascension of Christ, it can quickly become a devotional "optional extra," and cease to communicate dimensions of the universal and cosmic transformation of all creation in Christ. In the light of the ascension in which the presence and activity of Christ is viewed, however, belief in the assumption of the Mother of Christ, body and soul, into heaven cannot but continue to inspire a fresh hearing of this exhortation from the Letter to the Colossians:

> So if you have been raised with Christ, seek the things that are above, where Christ is, seated at the right hand of God. Set your minds on things that are above, not on things that are on earth, for you have died, and your life is hidden with Christ in God. When Christ who is your

life is revealed, then you also will be revealed with him in glory. (Col 3:1–4)

CONCLUSION

The mystery of the ascension of Christ is especially challenging for an integral ecology. The risen Christ ascends beyond the familiar world of human experience into the fathomless depths of God and suggests dimensions of creation transformed. In an obvious sense, such a theology necessarily proceeds "by way of negation" if the believing mind is to break free from the myths and mundane images that tend to infect common understandings of the resurrection and the ascension. And yet, there is the overwhelming positivity of expectation: the Christ who has departed this world is to return, in the fullness of his evidence. Such an expectant longing does not leave Christian faith and its attendant mysticism merely in a zone of always-increasing negation. Whatever the distortions and deficiencies that theology and prayer must transcend, whatever the limitations inherent in concepts and images that must be acknowledged to negate and surpass them, there is no question of renouncing the expectation of Christ's return—however incalculable that might be.

In the light of the ascension, faith inhabits the in-between of Christ's departure and eventual return. Christ, as the form and measure of all creation, returns, but not as coming from outside the world of the present. It is truer to say that he returns *from within this world*. Within this world and on this earth, the Word was incarnate, and here lived and preached and died. In him, this world is risen and ascended, anticipating its final form when Christ, as the depth, coherence, and completion of all creation, will return.

We can foster an appropriate understanding of what God is revealing in the ascension by making connections between its various aspects—trinitarian, christological, pneumatological, ecclesiological, sacramental, mystical, ecological, and so forth. In that way, theology can suggest a certain synthesis in its effort to say something positive in accord with its hope. We need not remain tongue-tied in looking to Christ's return and the eschatological consummation of all things in God. Indeed, we can think of the ascension in its relationship to the expanding event of the incarnation, and thus preclude the tendency to think of the ascension as the disembodiment, dehumanization, or "excarnation" of Christ. The continuance and expansion of the incarnation, when so understood, has profound ecclesiological, eschatological, and ecological significance.

Because of the ascension, elemental notions such as "world," "heaven," "time," and "place" need to be recast. If Christ has ascended in his humanity into heaven, then humanity and the world in which it is inextricably immersed has entered a new mode of existence. It is not as though Christ has left the world, but is now related to it in a new way—just our humanity has not been discarded in the ascended Christ. In this sense, heaven, in Christian terms, is not a vague celestial location but communion with God in Christ in a creation transformed. It is, in the words of Jesus in John's Gospel, "heaven opened," with "the angels of God ascending and descending upon the Son of Man" (John 1:51). Through Christ's ascension to the Father, a new age of communication between God and the world is inaugurated. In Christ, the world has been irreversibly taken up into the life of God, and God has come down into the life of the world. It is no longer a matter of fitting Christ into an unredeemed world, or of envisioning him disappearing into a vaguely determined heaven. Rather, the challenge consists in seeing both the world and heaven embodied in him: something new has begun; time and space are newly configured when the ascended Christ is the center and the focus of God's action and the scope of an integral ecology.

CHAPTER 6

Befriending Death

I N THIS CHAPTER, we consider death—an obvious dimension of life on this planet and a condition for its evolution—in its relation to integral ecology. When ecology veers toward ideological refusal to give death its due, there is little room for an "integral ecology." More seriously, if the way death is either suffered or inflicted in this terrestrial existence is not acknowledged, it can feed into the "culture of death" that Pope John Paul lamented (as opposed to a culture of life and true flourishing).[1]

There are four headings shaping what follows:

1. The Deadliness of Death;
2. From Denial to Surrender;
3. The Moment of Truth; and
4. Before the Foundation of the World.

THE DEADLINESS OF DEATH

Not to reflect deeply on the reality of death in the present ecological context can have fateful consequences, especially when it appears that the human species itself is so inherently destructive—of itself and of other species on the planet. Given the wars, the violence, oppression, rivalries existing between human beings, and the manic production of weapons of destruction of all kinds, it may be unwise to suggest that humans love other species on this planet as we love ourselves. Further, it is hard to pretend to any ecological integrity when abortion is prevalent to a degree that would cause alarm if it occurred in other species. Similarly, from an ecological perspective, the chemical manipulation of the human reproductive systems has proceeded too long unexamined in its long-term effects. After all, through sexuality, nature is experienced in its most entrancing, creative, and beautiful embodiment. It cannot be dismissed from ecological consideration.

Huge moral questions concern the pollution of the inner culture of human existence when consumerism takes hold of the human psyche. An integral ecology must allow for considerations that are deeper than the purely empirical interactions or routine social and cultural activities. What is at stake is a comprehensive ecological view of the fullness of life. In this respect, death must be given its due as an obvious fact of experience, in the inevitable succession of generations through birth and death as generation follows generation in all life on earth.[2] The focus on how ecology can profit from an acceptance of death is the question. For instance, it has been argued that a primal fear of death lies behind the culture of consumerism and the individual lifestyles it inspires.

We must give death its due if we are to appreciate the beauty and wonder of terrestrial life. Pope Francis has issued a robust denunciation of consumerism. His sensitivity to the sufferings of the earth and its people, his lamentation over the disappearance of so many species of fauna and flora, and his special reference to the deaths of the poor and infants (*LS* 20, 20, 48), are all evidences of a sober realism. Nonetheless, there is little explicit mention of death in his encyclical. Indeed, he does not include in his citation of the "Canticle of St. Francis" the verse the saint added as his own death approached: "Be praised my Lord through our Sister Bodily Death, from whose embrace no living person can escape." In the interests of a genuine integral ecology, therefore, this chapter considers the ecological and theological significance of death for appreciating and protecting the wonder of life on this planet. Downplaying the reality of death may lead to a superficial ecology sustained merely by a naïve or romantic optimism.

After a century and a half of evolutionary science, we can begin to understand the randomness, contingency, and terrible costs of evolution in the 3.8 billion-year history of life on this planet. At that point, a theology of the Crucified Christ will have a special relevance, deferring to hope in Christ crucified and risen for a deeper appreciation of "Sister Death" in the universe of God's creation.[3] An integral ecology must insist on including the fact and mystery of death in the interdisciplinary collaborative framework it envisages.

Ecological destruction of planetary proportions is the subject of widespread lament and anxiety. In contrast, there is another sense of diminishment in the words of the Johannine Jesus: "Unless a grain of wheat falls into the earth and dies, it remains just a single grain; but if it dies, it bears much fruit" (John 12:24). Here, an inevitable and even positive sense of diminishment is subsumed into the ultimate hope for transformation and communion. In the language of hope, death and dying have an essential place in life and so serve the purposes of the "sublime communion" (LS 89) that the Creator is bringing about.

The fact and reality of death permits no theoretical synthesis of the psychological, philosophical, theological, and ecological actors involved.[4] Nonetheless, the following headings in this chapter can serve to deepen reflection and sharpen conscience.

From one point of view, death is a matter-of-fact biological reality, necessarily inscribed into the dynamics of evolution. There can be no evolutionary progress unless death ensures the succession of generations. It is the price to be paid for the evolution of life on earth, making possible the emergence of differentiated, complex living beings in a world of wonderful biodiversity. Unless we belong to the mortal world of life on this planet, human beings would never have come into existence.[5]

Moreover, there is a sober, scientific backdrop to the death of individuals and species, the eventual collapse of the solar system, even if billions of years from now. And that will entail the extinction of all life on this planet. Indeed, cosmic events that have been lethal to planetary life in the past can reoccur. In a scientific account of catastrophes in this life-bearing universe, William R. Stoeger, SJ, considers the probabilities within a timeframe of fifty million years—enough time for the appearance and disappearance of a species.[6] Though planetary death can be remote from any present consideration because of the long-term timescale involved, it is nonetheless certain to happen. In such a case, the character of the cosmos as life-bearing would be extinguished. For Christian faith and hope, however, it would provoke renewed theological reflection on the resurrection of the body and what the new creation—the new heavens and the new earth—might possibly mean.

In the meantime, we can reflect on how life and death belong to the very heart of creation.[7] The law of entropy is built into the cosmos itself. All systems break down and the fundamental chaos finally takes over. Dispassionate scientific objectivity points irreversibly in that direction.

An integral ecology, on the one hand, must include a range of scientific conclusions on the inevitable death of the universe. On the other hand, it highlights the wonder of life and all the varied lifeforms that have appeared—in their improbable contingency. To this degree, *data* begin to appear as *dona*, and call forth gratitude to a giver for the gift of sheer existence. We will take up this idea specifically in a later chapter dealing with ecology and eschatology.

In the meantime, though, human history has always known its catalog of natural disasters, famines, earthquakes, plagues—"acts of God." We now live with the eerie possibility of death-dealing human activities affecting the planet in the era of the Anthropocene. Biological warfare, thermonuclear incineration, and ecological destruction still menace life on this planet. Huge technological systems shape the ecological, social, political, and economic world. The consumerist economy is insatiable in its demands. Enormous military arsenals at the disposition of dozens of governments openly include weapons of mass destruction designed for biological or thermonuclear warfare. This range of lethal capacities is the material expression of a readiness to wipe out whole populations if the necessity arises. Given that the possibilities of megadeath are taken for granted in the contemporary environment, the task of an integral ecology must at least be to mitigate the probabilities of global self-destruction and to promote a disarmament of the heart, and the kinds of reconciliation that can remove environmental threats from our common home. The spiritual task is to draw attention to the ultimate horizon of the mystery of life, its source and goal.

FROM DENIAL TO SURRENDER

A dread of death goes some way in explaining morbid aspects of modern culture. Obsessive consumerism, deracinated individualism, and careless destruction of the environment alike arise from the failure to give death its due. Ernest Becker expresses the thesis of his now-classic work, *The Denial of Death*: "The idea of death, the fear of it, haunts the human animal like nothing else; it is the mainspring of human activity—activity designed largely to avoid the fatality of death, to overcome it by denying in some way that it is the final destiny for man."[8] All are confronted with the question of the significance of the natural world, as it includes ourselves, all living things, and even the existence of our planetary home. Inevitably, all this is on the way to death. Becker recalls us from a primordial psychological terror in the face of death to a radical acceptance of creaturehood. As creatures, we are immersed in the totality of nature, connected to it, caught up and carried along by it. Authentic life arises only by accepting the limitation and contingency of our existence within this universe, and yielding ourselves into the stream of life and death.

In this respect, religious experience is essentially a "creature feeling" in the face of the massive transcendence of creation, and within the overwhelming miracle of the universe. The human person is caught between inevitable limitations and openness to the uncanny gift of life and existence in the world as it is.[9] On the one hand, the perspective of an integral ecology exposes what Becket has named the "vital lie" of culture built on the denial of death.[10] On the other hand, facing the reality of death leads to a deeper and more wonderful participation in the mystery of life. Consequently, genuine authenticity is attained only through the courageous acceptance of creatureliness. In a more philosophical and religious range of sensibility, Becker writes, "By being or doing, we fashion something, an object or ourselves, and drop it into the confusion, make an offering of it, so to speak, to the life-force."[11] The challenge is to a lived sense of relationality, and to exercise the virtues of praise and thankfulness that are at the heart of religious faith.

A shared sense of the human condition promises renewed collaboration between science and religion. Science improperly absorbs

106

all truth into itself, as has been already pointed out. Religious faith, consequently, leads to a larger version of truth. It enables human beings to be open toward the miracle and mystery. Living the truth of creation, human beings would be less driven to undo themselves, and be more conformed to the image of God, as they live in harmony with the rest of creation.[12] Becker anticipates the ecological crisis of today by noting that those whose awareness is shaped by what is in effect the living truth of an integral ecology "would be less likely to poison the rest of creation."[13]

Faith is contemplative in its reverent openness to the mystery of creation and the Creator. It exercises, also, a redemptive effect in causing human beings to be less driven to self-destruct, and more disposed to realize the divine image in the works of love and justice. More to the point, the religious sense of the Creator and creation is of ecological value, in that it demands living in harmony with "the rest of creation," and lessens the likelihood of poisoning it. Most of all, a genuinely creaturely consciousness relativizes the harmful effects of the "denial of death." To come to a point of healing is to accept our puniness in the face of the overwhelming majesty of the universe, to become aware of the unspeakable miracle of even a single living being, and so begin to waken to the chaotic depths of the immense, inconclusive drama of creation.[14] The authentic self, therefore, is realized in its connectedness with all creation. It might be fittingly termed the "ecological" or "cosmic" self—that is, the *religious* self as just described, bonded to the Creator and all creation—in contrast to the tiny scope of the fear-driven, illusory self, fabricated by denying death. The true self is realized only by befriending the mortal character of existence.

Consequently, authenticity consists in attaining or regaining the virtue of humility, with its sense of the radical finitude and creatureliness.[15] Humility rests on the existential fact that spiritual life is earthed, grounded, bound up with the immense dynamism of nature into whose processes we are each and all immersed.[16] In the catalog of moral virtues, humility is a quality of freedom. It is shown in a radical decentering of the self, in the recognition that all is given, and that existence is a gift. In this respect, humility enables human consciousness to deal honestly and creatively with the dread of death by recognizing oneself as a creature within the mystery of the vast and uncanny universe.

Humility connects us to the whole, immersing each and all in a wondrous universe of gifts and giving. If ecological virtue is to be more than posturing, the cultivation of humility forms a basic attitude regarding life and creation. Out of humble acceptance of mortality and the decentering of the self can come the wisdom to coexist on this planet as "our common home." Life remains a question within an overwhelmingly uncanny universe. It is most clear that none of us is the center of that universe, for we have emerged out of a vast cosmic process and are dying back into it. When we begin to ask about the true center, the true life force of this overwhelming universe, an acceptance of self as mortal and finite is the beginning. It finds expression in humility, a "kenotic" attitude of self-surrender in life and in death. There follows, if not adoration precisely, at least surrender to the unnamed, incomprehensible creative generosity at the origin of all being and life. Only a decentered self, conscious of its limitation, can live from and for a larger mystery, and in an integral ecology.

And yet there is a shadow. Death is shrouded in a darkness deeper than the inevitable termination of biological life. Death, Paul declares, is the "wages of sin" (Rom 6:23). The implication is that death is the consequence and manifestation of sin as alienation from God, and the refusal of communion—with the Creator, and creation. It is the choice for self-centered ego against all others. As a result, the seemingly natural fact of death becomes the carrier of a profound sense of rupture and guilt. It looms through life as "the last enemy" (1 Cor 15:26).[17]

Human culture is infected with the bias of "original sin."[18] We are born into a world skewed from its center and disrupted in the communion that God intends. In an alienated world, death is experienced as menacing and meaningless. Life and death are locked in an absurd conflict, with death assured of victory. The transcendent otherness of God and the created otherness of our neighbor and the world itself cannot but appear as a threat. The more human existence is turned in on itself, the more it occupies a shrinking universe. Consequently, human identity is formed in competitive self-assertion against the Other. In this respect, death is the deepest threat. Death holds no promise of life; it is the carrier of all that is meaningless and threatening to the life we have chosen and made.[19]

THE MOMENT OF TRUTH

The idea of death as the wages of sin invites a further application to ecological issues. Environmental destruction is brought about by human greed and carelessness, resulting in the death of species and loss of biodiversity, to say nothing of lethal effects on the lives of the poor. Death experienced as the wages of sin invites a deeper appreciation of the death of Christ and of Christian participation in his death and resurrection. More generally, illusions born of the denial of death cannot be total. Life contests the reign of death as total, for ordinary lives know sudden impulses of wonder, nameless hope, and the exhilaration of great loves, just as all are humbled before the strange grandeur of moral achievement. In such moments, there is an uncanny, death-resistant "more" in the experience of the mystic, the artist, the martyr, the prophet, the thinker, the scientist, and the activist. There is an intimation of eternity in the making, of "eternity coming to be as time's own mature fruit."[20]

Here, Ladislaus Boros's *The Moment of Truth: Mysterium Mortis* takes up where Becker's denial of death ends.[21] Empirically, death implies dissolution. But there is another dimension intimated in conscious experience: "whether this complete removal from self which we undergo in death does not conceal a much more fundamental process which could be described…in terms of the progressive achievement of selfhood, of actively initiating the self to life."[22] A positive hermeneutics of mortality based on a phenomenology of existence suggests that the thrust of human life is toward fulfillment—*in*, and even *through*, death. In dying, an individual existence moves to the bounds of its being. It awakes to a kind of full knowledge and liberty. The dynamics of personal existence that moved and motivated life in its normal course have been largely hidden from consciousness, only to surface at the moment of death into full awareness. The full dimensions of our being unfold.[23] In this respect, the self dies out of the limited individuality of the ego, into a more deeply relational form of being. This is to become aware of itself within the universal whole. This new form of consciousness registers "all at once and all together the universe that [the human person] has always borne hidden within himself, the universe with which he is already most intimately united, and which, one way or another, was always being produced from within him."[24] And yet, this unfolding is most deeply a meeting with God, the boundless Other who has been present in every stirring of existence. The deepest mystery of the Creator has worked within all the elements and causes that have formed us, our earth, our universe.[25] In the light of God, we are brought to a moment of final decision, whether to accept God and the totality of creation, allowing ourselves to be carried along by the flood of life, and being and belonging, toward an eternal fulfillment.[26]

Boros dramatically evokes the moment of final decision as the ultimate opportunity to crystallize one's life in a completely personal act. Paradoxically, it is our most fully conscious and free moment. It faces us with the decision—to choose life and the God of life for whom we were made. All in all, art, mysticism, love, and intelligence are promises that are yet to be kept. In death, the self-transcending movement of our existence will find its ultimate point of rest and its final vindication.[27]

The eschatological realization of the self in the presence of God the Creator is not incompatible with the realization of the self as coexistential with all God's creation. Going to God does not mean merely escaping from the earthly existence in which we lived and in which Christ has been our earthly brother. Rather, fulfillment in heaven must include this earth redeemed, transformed, and brought to fulfillment in God, all in all.

Here, Christ, crucified and risen, is the focus of faith and hope in the all-creative mystery of compassionate and transforming love. The death of Jesus was indeed deadly. It occurred as failure, betrayal, isolation, condemnation, torture, and execution. God's love felt the force of the human problem of evil. However, the love that gave itself to the end (John 13:1) was not defeated by the power of evil.[28] For the death of the crucified Jesus enacts and embodies the ultimate form of life as he surrenders himself to the Father in solidarity with the defeated and the lost. The ultimate point of Christ's self-offering reveals God as a love stronger than death. In Christ, crucified and risen, those receptive to the divine Gift are summoned to pass from a self-serving existence into the

God-centered realm of eternal life, already inaugurated in the gifts that will last—faith, hope, and love (see 1 Cor 13:13).

Death also remains as the limit of this form of earthly life, but then transformed into an act of ultimate self-surrender—to the Father in union with Christ, and in the creativity of the Spirit. Death becomes the way into participation in a larger vitality and communion. The entropy affecting each individual biological existence is dissipated to allow for a higher realization of communion, in relationship to the "all" and participation in the whole. The individual self becomes a wave of communion, a truly relational self. The upward vector of ascent for the human being moves from electrons, to atoms, to molecules, to proteins, to cells, to organisms, to the complexity of the human brain, and to the cosmic overture of human consciousness. In all this, the direction of life is one of transformation in increasingly rich and complex relationships. In this respect, death cannot mean terminal dissolution but rather the expansion of the self into its fullest relationality. Death would not be an alien intruder, but a relative—"Sister Death," as St. Francis could pray—within cosmic promise of the fullness of life in Christ.

Only a transformation of our whole embodied existence can answer the hopes written into life. By participating in his rising from the tomb, the entropy and limiting individuality of biological life is definitively overcome. A new creation is anticipated in Christ, "the resurrection and the life" (John 11:25). The realism of this new creation is expressed in all four Gospel narratives in regard to the empty tomb. It is the historical marker of the cosmic transformation that has begun in Christ:[29] "So if anyone is in Christ, there is a new creation: everything old has passed away; see, everything has become new!" (2 Cor 5:17).

Hope nonetheless remains hope. It lives always in the in-between of what is and what is yet to be, as it waits on the mystery of final transformation. Even the New Testament writer soberly concedes, "As it is, we do not yet see everything in subjection to them [the angels]" (Heb 2:8). Yet for all the sobriety of Christian hope, the great conviction remains firm. In Christ, the universe has been changed. Death has been radically "Christened." Christ did not die out of the world, but into it, to become its innermost coherence and dynamism. Indeed, in his death, resurrection, and ascension, the mystery of the incarnation is complete. For the Christian, dying in Christ is to be conformed to the crucified and risen One, in order to be newly embodied in the future form of cosmos itself:[30] "The last enemy to be destroyed is death....When all things are subjected to him, then the Son himself will also be subjected to him who put all things in subjection under him, that God may be all in all" (1 Cor 15:26–28).

All mortal existence is poised, therefore, over an abyss of life. The empty tomb, a sign of the creative power of the Spirit, is of cosmic significance.[31] It suggests the full-bodied reality of resurrection, and seeds history with questions and wonder as to what great transformation is afoot. The empty tomb, so soberly recorded in each of the four Gospels, offers no salvation in mere emptiness. It functions as a factor within the awakening of faith as a new consciousness of life unfolds. It moves, first, from the empty tomb, discovered as a puzzling fact. It then awakens to cosmic surprise over what had happened, for Jesus appears as newly and wonderfully alive: "Do not be afraid; I am the first and the last, and the living one. I was dead, and see, I am alive forever and ever" (Rev 1:17–18). Then faith returns to the tomb as an emblem of the new creation. From there it expands into the limitless horizons of a transformation of all things in Christ. Such faith is not primarily looking back at a death, but facing forward into the promise of eternal life, in a universe transformed.

BEFORE THE FOUNDATION OF THE WORLD

In the meantime, we are confronted with the agony of the world and the cost of evolution, with its deaths, extinctions, violence, and dead ends: "the whole creation has been groaning in labor pains until now" (Rom 8:22). Side by side with the cosmic cooperation that enables the evolutionary process, "competition, pain, and death [are] intrinsic to evolutionary processes."[32] Yet, the New Testament addresses the mystery of pain, suffering, death, and human failure without hesitation, in the light of the death, burial, and resurrection of Jesus (see 1 Cor 15:3–19). In this light, human beings can accept this planetary existence and their responsibilities within it. An integral ecology learns from the ecological sciences to appreciate the varied wonder of life, to mourn the extinctions that have occurred, and to lament over the lethal agents at work in the environment of human society and culture. But despair is premature. The special energies of Christian hope are ever-renewable resources.

The Christian theology informing integral ecology is focused in the paschal realism of Christ's death and resurrection. It offers no supertheory to explain death away. Questions remain. First, is our theology sufficiently humble? There can be no theological theory or ecological system that controls death, nor any egomaniac subjectivity able to appropriate death to its purposes. Inscribed into the course of our lives is an elemental rupture; any expression of hope that represses the lethal force of death is not starting from scratch. A beauteous sense of nature or the wonder of the universe unfolding through its billions of years cannot camouflage the finality of death in all living things. Even theologians may find themselves offering a guided tour of the world of eschatological fulfillment, but to no avail. In the face of death, all must "wait in a condition of openness toward miracle and mystery, in the lived truth of creation."[33]

In other words, are we really letting ourselves and others—even Jesus himself—really die? In our Easter celebrations, we may have been too inclined to hurry past the caesura of Holy Saturday. The liturgy graphically portrays this in the stripping of the altars and emptiness of the tabernacle. It drives home a basic truth: before death can mean resurrection, it must mean being dead—even for Jesus himself. He went down into the realm of the dead, as in the words of the Apostles' Creed, he "descended into hell." The Crucified was dead and buried. Christian hope is not a video replay of highlights once the team has won. In Holy Saturday, a healing providence makes time for all our human griefs and lamentations, in a world of apparent God-forsakenness, failure, and waiting for God to act in God's appropriate time; in God's own way. Jesus was not only dead, but buried, descended to the depths of universal dread. To hurry past the deadly reality of the cross to a kind of automatic resurrection would obscure the need for a time of waiting before that Friday can be affirmed as "Good" and that Saturday as "Holy." Only by waiting on that unfolding can the imagination be christened, and hope expand beyond repressive optimism to its authentically God-centered character.[34]

The horizon of hope is shaped by Christ's self-giving unto death for the sake of the world's salvation. This gift occurs so that "by the grace of God he might taste death for everyone" (Heb 2:9), and "free those who all their lives were held in slavery by the fear of death" (Heb 2:15). In the gift of Christ, a multidimensioned giving is at work: Christ gives himself in death for the salvation of the world, and the Father so loves the world as to give the Son into such a death (Rom 8:32; John 3:16). The gift of the Spirit breathes faith into the mortal existence of Christ's followers: "Those who believe in me, even though they die, will live" (John 11:25). The crucified and living One embodies the ultimate life-form: "I am the first and the last, and the living one. I was dead, and see, I am alive forever and ever; and I have the keys of Death and of Hades" (Rev 1:17–18).

Though hope relies on the God whose love is stronger than death, it has the realism to admit that "in the days of his flesh, Jesus offered up prayers and supplications, with loud cries and tears, to the one who was able to save him from death" (Heb 5:7). The God of life has acted. But the Father did not save Jesus from death, but vindicated and glorified him in his death for others by raising him to a new order of life. As the form and source of new life, he is the firstborn from the dead (Col 1:18). In the light of his death, hope looks through death and beyond it. But it does so, first, by being a way into it—in union with Christ in his death: "Since, therefore, the children share flesh and blood, he himself likewise shared the same things, so that through death he might destroy the one who has the power of death" (Heb 2:14). To be united with him in his death is to share his victory over all the demonic forces that work in human culture—and, consequently, in the environment, through the threat of death. By sharing in his death, hope is already sharing in his resurrection (see Rom 6:3–5). Still, hope remains hope. It is never immune to the darkness of life. It must show its own patience. It means waiting for the mystery of love to prove itself stronger than death and all the demonic powers that use the threat of death for their purposes. The New Testament expresses a sober realism:

As it is, we do not yet see everything in subjection to them, but we do see Jesus, who for a little while was made lower than the angels, now crowned with glory and honor because of the suffering of death, so that by the grace of God he might taste death for everyone. (Heb 2:8–9)

There is a further edge at which theology trembles: the mystery of God. Though the holy and immortal God does not die, there is something about the way God is God, about the way the Trinity is these three self-giving divine persons, that leads death into the deepest darkness of all. This deeper darkness is not a threat, but an intimation of life in its trinitarian and most vital dimensions. Union with Christ in his death is most radically self-abandonment to the Father. It yields to the incalculable creativity of the life-giving Spirit. It means incorporation in the Body of Christ. In this trinitarian frame of reference, a self-surrender is inevitably asked of each mortal being. But that is to share in the unreserved self-emptying of the Divine Three in relation to each other, and to the world they have created and drawn into their communal life. Death, in this respect, is the last, and perhaps the only truly genuine act of adoration of the God whose life is self-giving love. Only by dying out of the cultural and biological systems and projects structuring this present existence are human beings remade in conformity with the self-giving and communal trinitarian life of God. Ghislain Lafont notes that dying in Christ means a recentering of our existence along truly personal lines. "Autonomous existence within the world yields to an unbroken life of communion with God, and with all [creation] in God."[35]

In conclusion, a consideration of death makes for a more integral ecology, and such an integral ecology makes for a deeper understanding of "Sister Death."

CHAPTER 7

Ecology and Eschatology

POPE FRANCIS IN his encyclical *Laudato Si'* treats of the ecology of planet Earth in a way that necessarily provokes an eschatological consideration of "our common home."[1] In the language of Christian hope, this present world, in which Jesus of Nazareth is the Word incarnate, will be transformed into a new creation, and all things will attain their plenitude in Christ. How should we understand the transformation of nature where "lives the dearest freshness deep down things"?[2] More precisely, the Word, in becoming flesh, assumed human nature: with us and like us, he is an "earthling." When Christian hope speaks of "the resurrection of the body" and a "new creation" in Christ, it provokes this question: Does such hope extend to the terrestrial constitution and planetary milieu of our bodily being, even if no detailed description can be given? Any attempted answer belongs to the rhetoric of hope focused on the Word incarnate, crucified and risen. Given that "what we will be has not yet been revealed" (1 John 3:2), the best we can do is to sketch the following four avenues of approach to this question for the sake of stimulating further discussion and an ever-larger hope. The first and overall consideration is the horizon of hope itself.

THE RANGE OF HOPE

The words of the pope are full of hope, even if they outstrip our theological capacities. He writes,

> At the end, we will find ourselves face to face with the infinite beauty of God (cf. *1 Cor* 13:12), and be able to read with admiration and happiness the mystery of the universe, which with us will share in unending pleni-tude. Even now we are journeying towards the sabbath of eternity, the new Jerusalem, towards our common home in heaven. Jesus says: "I make all things new" (*Rev* 21:5). Eternal life will be a shared experience of awe, in which each creature, resplendently transfigured, will take its rightful place and have something to give those poor men and women who will have been liberated once and for all. (*LS* 243)

Such rhetorical expression presumes some clear points:

- Beatific vision is of God, yet it somehow includes an understanding of the mystery of the created universe in which we participate.[3]
- All are moving toward a new creation in Christ.
- Eternal life will be a shared experience in which the wonder of each transfigured creature will come into its own, and be a gift to liberated human beings.[4]

The vision of the infinite beauty of God characterizes eschato-logical fulfillment. The doctrinal tradition of the "beatific vision" is therefore specified as beholding the infinite beauty of the Creator and the God-given wonder of the universe itself. Human beings, along with all creation, will share in an unsurpassable fulfillment and plenitude of being in God. Already, creation is moving in this direction, destined to arrive at the heavenly city (Rev 21:2) and "our common home." The words of Jesus, "I make all things new"

(Rev 21:5), witness to the power of his resurrection as it flows into creation, with Christ himself the source and form of eternal life. Eternal life cannot but be a shared experience of universal delight, when all creation is transfigured as the "hungry are filled with good things, and the lowly are lifted up" (see Luke 1:52–53).

Pope Francis goes on to say,

> In the meantime, we come together to take charge of this home which has been entrusted to us, knowing that all the good which exists here will be taken up into the heavenly feast. In union with all creatures, we journey through this land seeking God, for "if the world has a beginning and if it has been created, we must enquire who gave it this beginning and who was its Creator."[5] Let us sing as we go. May our struggles and our concern for this planet never take away the joy of our hope. (*LS* 244)

We note the following points:

- This all-inclusive hope has practical consequences in a greater ecological responsibility.
- All the goodness we have known will be part of the eschatological banquet—though, we might add, without any connotation of consumerism!
- As human beings, we must press on in union with all created realities, seeking the Creator revealed in all creation.
- The mood of this movement toward the end is one of hopeful joy.

The pope's call to environmental responsibility, even in the face of the destruction inflicted on God's good creation, remains hopeful.[6] Hope finds consolation in the thought that nothing is lost, and that all that is good will feature in the heavenly banquet. The journey of the universe is one of vast companionship. In moving toward the end, we carry the world with us, individually and collectively. Although the environmental crisis is of planetary proportions, hope in God already occupies the future in the making by stretching forward to that Omega point where God will be "all in all" (1 Cor 15:28).[7]

How, then, might this hope anticipate the eschatological fulfillment of this world of God's creation and human habitation?[8] Pope Francis's words echo in many ways the unprecedented and evocative declaration of Vatican II's *Gaudium et Spes* fifty years earlier:

> We do not know the time for the consummation of the earth or of humanity, nor do we know how all things will be transformed. As deformed by sin, the shape of this world will pass away; but we are taught that God is preparing a new dwelling place and a new earth where justice will abide, and whose blessedness will answer and surpass all the longings for peace which spring up in the human heart. Then, with death overcome, the sons of God will be raised in Christ, and what was sown in weakness and corruption will be invested with incorruptibility. Enduring with charity and its fruits, all that creation which God made on man's account will be unchained from the bondage of vanity. (*Gaudium et Spes* 39)

Admittedly, this passage lacks the ecological loading of *Laudato Si'*, being more anthropocentric in its outlook and in line with the humanism pervading the conciliar document. The ecological question is not the critical issue it has become. "The Church in the Modern World" had to find its way as "the Church in the postmodern world" before it could become "the Church in the ecological world of planet Earth." If this evolutionary world is to be subjected to the power of the resurrection, what kind of environment might eschatological hope envisage? Even though a guided tour of the world to come is not available, it is time to reconsider such issues.

Some twenty years ago, Peter Phan wrote a comprehensive and even prophetic article appealing to the passage just cited from *Gaudium et Spes*.[9] His treatment of the somewhat muted "ecological motif" in the theological tradition led to a consideration of the basic metaphors and models that have been at work at various stages of the theological tradition (cf. H. Paul Santmire). He notes also the inclusive power of a "common creation story" beginning with the Big Bang (cf. Sallie McFague). He concludes with words of striking relevance:

> Theologians may be reluctant to describe in detail how the material cosmos and everything in it will endure and be transformed lest they be accused of indulging in fanciful ruminations. But it is high time, given the current ecological crisis, to underscore as forcefully as possible the symbiotic relationship between humans and the environment and to affirm unambiguously that without the permanence of the physical cosmos, on which they depend for their material and spiritual survival and for which they must care by means of ecologically responsible actions, humans cannot achieve that eternal happiness for which their hearts long.[10]

The philosophical and theological accounts of creation are quite compatible with the recent scientific theory of the Big Bang. On the one hand, it would be disastrous for any theology of creation to reduce itself to this one scientific model as the exclusive foundation of a common creation story. From a theological point of view, the only reality that created beings have in common is their Creator. Perhaps, too, some version of the "Steady State Theory" might reemerge, or the Big Bang theory might be located within some kind of cosmic oscillation of expansion and contraction. Theologians must remain open to scientific exploration. On the other hand, to reduce all creation, from archangels to wombats, to say nothing of the human spirit, to the potentiality of the Big Bang as the beginning of time and space seems monodimensionally materialistic. The mystery of creation does not envisage God as a pretemporal pyrotechnician igniting a cosmic firecracker. The primary image focusing theological exploration is not an unimaginable explosive event, but the theopoetic Word: "and God said, 'Let there be....'" The divine Word is freely creative of *this* world, out of an infinity of divine possibilities. If science continues to the find the Big Bang as the most plausible model for cosmic beginnings, theology must learn what it can. Since God created a spatio-temporal world, then its genesis would no doubt look something like the way in which contemporary physics is describing it. God does not have to be factored into the physical explanation as a specific, categorical cause, but, as Creator, God is the cause operating in all causality and creativity, the "transcendent" cause as the philosophical tradition would name it. A theological understanding of creation implies adoration of the Creator, while the Big Bang is a plausible scientific hypothesis. Creation is about the totality of gracious mystery implied in every "now," while the Big Bang is about a mathematically imagined "then." The creed's confession of the Creator of all things, visible and invisible, is not reducible to a scientific model of cosmic emergence and evolutionary development. Faith in creation is about how everything depends on God, whereas the Big Bang is about the common emergence of the material cosmos from an original event occurring 13.8 billion years ago. Creation tells the story of the eternal God who acts in freedom and love to call the universe into existence, while the Big Bang is about the beginning of a temporal and spatial cosmic reality, the singularity of a physical and mathematically computed event, and its resultant dynamic structure. Finally, creation is about abiding mystery, while the Big Bang is about the most plausible solution to the problem of cosmic origins. In short, creation implies a holistic sense of how all being, intelligence, value, and beauty derive from, and lead to, the mystery of the Creator.[11] In contrast, the Big Bang is an elegant mathematical formulation of material emergence, a protolanguage of cosmic origins.

A theological sense of creation cannot risk "indulging in fanciful ruminations," as Phan warns. Nevertheless, we can touch on two biblical topics deserving of further exploration.

TWO BIBLICAL PERSPECTIVES

From Garden to City

First, it is seldom remarked that, biblically speaking, creation begins with a garden (see Genesis), and ends in a city (see Revelation). To that degree, there is no need to romanticize a rural existence or yearn for unspoiled nature. The human vocation to tend the original garden of creation moves to a God-given completion in the city of the new Jerusalem coming down from heaven.

John the Seer writes,

> Then I saw a new heaven and a new earth; for the first
> heaven and the first earth had passed away, and the sea
> was no more. And I saw the holy city, the new Jerusa-
> lem, coming down out of heaven from God, prepared as
> a bride adorned for her husband. (Rev 21:1–2)

The voice from the throne promises that "death will be no more...
for the first things have passed away" (Rev 21:4). That city will
have no temple since its temple "is the Lord God...and the
Lamb....For the glory of God is its light, and its lamp is the Lamb"
as the liberated people of the earth "bring into it the glory and the
honor of the nations" (Rev 21:22–26). We gladly defer to biblical
scholarship for the full connotation of these terms, but this much
is clear.[12] In the new environment of the heavenly city, death will
be banished, and all will be revealed in the immediate light of
God and Christ.

In an eschatological and incarnational horizon, environmental
questions arise. After all, the risen Christ is not "excarnated," nor
has he ceased being an "earthling" in his expanding incarnation!
Since it is not as though he has become disembodied, it is better
for hope to admit that we human beings are not yet fully embodied—in Christ.[13] From this earthly point of view, the resurrection-
ascension of Christ is an expanding bodily event, in accord with
God's continuing incarnational action in the world. Accordingly,
Christ's risen existence continues, expands, and integrates his
communication in the body in a way that can affect us even now.
By partaking of the Body of Christ and participating in it, there is
new sight, hearing, touching, tasting, eating and drinking, feeling
and indwelling—the new senses of faith, as Origen recognized so
clearly.[14] Because of its unobjectifiable immediacy and mutuality,
the Body of Christ, head and members, is a zone of an intersubjectivity that "earths" and enfleshes faith's experience of the Risen
One. He is the source and form of the new creation in his all-
inclusive, corporate reality of Christ: "for you have died, and your
life is hidden with Christ in God. When Christ who is your life is
revealed, then you also will be revealed with him in glory" (Col
3:3–4). Believers are offered a new sense of corporate coexistence:

"In that renewal there is no longer Greek and Jew, circumcised and uncircumcised, barbarian, Scythian, slave and free; but Christ is all and in all" (Col 3:11).

The event of the incarnation of the Word on this earth has occurred, and this continues to expand throughout history.[15] Our understanding of the incarnation of the Word is extended not only to the evolutionary and ecological world, but also to the electronic or cyberspace dimensions of the world of communication, occurring through a kind of electronic "nervous system"—ideally at the service of human intelligence and a growing solidarity in world-shaping events. In anticipation of ultimate levels of unity and communion, the world itself has become the shared body of our being together to anticipate the ultimate city in which human beings will dwell.

The development of global communication suggests an analogy for the eschatological environment of the heavenly city. If the spirit of human inventiveness and creativity has so transformed our embodied terrestrial existence, how will the Holy Spirit, having already raised the Crucified One from the tomb and animated the risen Body of Christ, penetrate and transform all creation? Creation is not thereby dematerialized, nor disembodied, nor abrogated. The materiality of our existence is given back and restored by God as a gift, even though the reality of the glorified body eludes description. This is not the occasion to ponder the value of medieval speculation on the *dotes* of the Body of Christ in glory.[16] Such medieval concerns may appear somewhat quaint to the less imaginative and more secular outlook of today. Nevertheless, speculation on the eschatological environment associated with the new heavens and the new earth continues regarding the transformation of our bodies along with other terrestrial bodies. A larger vision is inspired to some degree by Pope Francis's *Laudato Si'*. The question arises, does this profusion of wonderful life forms and of all the variety of terrestrial beauty have no place in that future when God will be *panta en passin*, "all in all" (1 Cor 15:28)? Are the evolutionary dynamics of the world to have no effect in an eschatological environment of the New Jerusalem? Do death and decay, the universal feature of an evolutionary environment, preclude—as yet unimaginable—transformations of the animal, vegetable, and mineral world? How does one answer the inevitable heartfelt question, "Do our pets go to heaven?"[17]

From the Foundation of the World:
The Slain Lamb

There is a second perspective determined by the image of the Lamb slain from the foundation of the world, as though to communicate self-sacrifice on the part of God as primordially constitutive of creation itself. Ecological awareness cannot but be confronted with the agony of the world and the cost of evolution, with its deaths, extinctions, violence, and dead ends: "the whole of creation has been groaning in labor pains until now" (Rom 8:22). Though birth, not death, is the hope, Denis Edwards remarks that "competition, pain, and death [are] intrinsic to evolutionary processes."[18] In the agony and struggle inscribed in nature itself, we turn from the image of heavenly City to that of the Lamb that was slaughtered before the foundation of the world (see Rev 13:8; 5:6, 7–8, 11–12; 7:13–17; 12:11). It suggests an aboriginally self-sacrificial divine love that is constitutive of creation and providence. Aspects of a prevenient, self-giving love come to expression when Paul affirms that Christ Jesus emptied himself of "the form of God," to take on the form of a slave (Phil 2:5–7).[19] Likewise, in later Pauline developments, the Letter to the Colossians describes the Christ as "the image of the invisible God, the firstborn of all creation....He himself is before all things, and in him all things hold together" (Col 1:15, 17). Similarly, the Letter to the Ephesians proclaims, "He chose us in Christ before the foundation of the world to be holy and blameless before him in love" (Eph 1:4). At the foundation of Johannine Christology is the intimate union between the *Logos* with God that preexisted "the beginning" (John 1:1–2). In his final prayer, the Johannine Jesus prays to his Father that he might return to the glory that was his, in God's presence "before the world existed" (John 17:5).

Completing and intensifying these perspectives on God's primordial, prevenient, and sacrificial love is the vision of the slaughtered and risen Lamb shining into all the darkness and violence of history, "from the foundation of the world" (Rev 5:6; 13:8). This light penetrates even into the evolutionary *agōnia* of the cosmos,[20] given that suffering and death are a necessary part of the evolutionary process. In some sense, it follows that the struggles and ambiguities of creation that have occurred from the beginnings of time are already purified by the blood of the Lamb (Rev 7:13–17). The key element in the relationship of God to the world, that is, from "before the foundation of the world," has been the continuing presence of the crucified and risen One: "Do not be afraid; I am the first and the last, and the living one. I was dead, and see, I am alive forever and ever; and I have the keys of Death and of Hades" (Rev. 1:17b–18). As Moloney remarks,

> John the Seer introduces the crucified into that process, bringing God's healing, in and through his pre-existent Son, a Lamb slain before all time....Thus, that community faces its ambiguous reality with a hope founded in awareness that it has been cleansed by the blood of the slain Lamb since "before the foundation of the world."[21]

The New Testament addresses the mystery of pain, suffering, death, and human failure without hesitation, and, in the light of the death, burial, and resurrection of Jesus (see 1 Cor 15:3–19), looks to the new creation. Nor does this hope forget that the risen and glorified body of Jesus still bears the wounds of the cross.[22]

LOVE AND THE MULTIPLICITY OF CREATION

The two perspectives just outlined—the God-given city coming down from heaven in contrast to the human cultivation of a garden alone, and the Lamb slain before the foundation of the world as opposed to later remedial action—affect our thinking on the eschatological environment. A universal transformation is envisaged, but how that should be expressed, either protologically or eschatologically, is a daunting theological task. The transformation of the entirety of creation in Christ surpasses our present capacities to understand and imagine. Any vocabulary expressive of "the last things" environmentally or ecologically is doubly difficult. To offer some analogical understanding of what no eye has seen and no ear heard regarding the new heaven and the new earth, let alone any possible presence of flora and fauna in that state, is necessarily a speculative exercise (see Isa 11:6–9). Nonetheless, it is possible to anticipate the eschatological environment as a "sublime communion." The ever-creative mystery of God would be immediately experienced within the totality of creation in such a way that everything is appreciated as *quid Dei*, as an explicit manifestation of the divine. There are limitations. In routine experience, there is no imagining the cadences of a great poem just by opening a dictionary; no enjoyment of the splendor of great painting merely by looking at the artist's untidy palette. How the human spirit can transform into art the sounds, colors, and shapes pertaining to terrestrial realities remains mystery enough. But any notion of how the divine Spirit can penetrate this earthly realm and bring about the new heavens and new earth requires another dimension of the theological virtue of hope centered on the resurrection of the Crucified. How might God-given hope, therefore, envisage the end when God will be "all in all" (1 Cor 15:28)?

The Multiplicity of Creation

Aquinas's theology is deeply appreciative of the varied and precious particularities of creation. Here, we focus on two aspects: first, the significance of plurality in creation; and second, God's originating love regarding each being. Both aspects can be developed beyond the rather anthropocentric eschatology of the great medieval systems.[23]

First, then, regarding *the necessary plurality of created beings*, each element of creation has its own quasi-absolute value. It is a specific realization of the divine. The numinous sense of nature that so many ecologists bring to their commitments today is no doubt living from a subterranean connection with a great medieval vision, as when Aquinas writes,

> God planned to create many distinct things in order to
> share with them and reproduce in them his goodness.
> Because no one creature could do this, he produced many

126

diverse creatures, so that what was lacking in one expression of his goodness could be made up by another; for the goodness which is simply and wholly in God, is shared in by creatures in many different ways. Hence, the whole universe shares and expresses that goodness better than any individual creature.[24]

If, in terrestrial life, each creature manifests something of the goodness of God, one aspect of beatific vision must be, precisely and positively, to see how God is revealed in each being, and how each being explicitly manifests the beauty and wisdom of God in the great consummation when God is "all in all." Given that God is manifested in every creature, there is every reason to expect that the new creation would not entail such creatures ceasing to exist after this present terrestrial phase. A theology of the beatific vision of God, accordingly, must extend to God manifested in every detail of creation, but as transfigured in the environment of the new heavens and new earth.

To see God the Creator of the universe "face to face" is also to see God revealed and communicated in the whole span of creation. The beatific vision is not a matter of looking at God "from the outside," but is best conceived as a participative kind of knowing born of immersion in the boundless ocean of trinitarian life. It is to live from, with, and in God. In the words of St. Augustine, "After this life, God himself is where we will be" (*ipse* [*Deus*] *post istam vitam est locus noster*).[25] In the life of the world to come, our existence is no longer determined by evolutionary biology in the way we live and die in the ecology and environment of this planet. Our location, as Augustine suggests, will be God all in all, in an environment shaped and formed by God's self-communication to creation. Admittedly, the theological tradition understands the beatific vision as a divine communication without created intermediary. God is ultimately known only in the Divine Word: "In your light we see light" (Ps 36:9). But such a blissful immediacy surely enables the blessed to identify God in every aspect and element of the creation, and to find creation in its every element and aspect in God. Creation is thus immediately appreciated as the manifestation of the divine glory of love and beauty. Everything and everyone, therefore, will be seen to exist in God in a "sublime communion" (*LS* 89). Every element and aspect of the universe will be transformed so as to evidence in its own way the creative mystery of God. In that environment of the world transformed, the determining factor is the Father's "plan for the fullness of time, to gather up all things in him [Christ], things in heaven and things on earth" (Eph 1:10). In that christic[26] consummation, the ultimate environment is determined in ways beyond our present powers of imagination, for Christ is

> the image of the invisible God, the firstborn of all creation; for in him all things in heaven and on earth were created, things visible and invisible, whether thrones or dominions or rulers or powers—all things have been crated through him and for him. He himself is before all things, and in him all things hold together. (Col 1:15–17)

The Creativity of Love

Creation, in its variety and unity, not only shares in the beauty and goodness of the Creator, but is brought into existence by an act of free creative and eternal love.[27] This is to say that the being and variety of creation stands forth as total gift. In this respect, God's love is not first attracted toward some good object already existing, but it is the divine loving that causes it to exist. Everything, insofar as it exists, has been loved into existence by the divine freedom: "the love of God is pouring in and creating goodness in things" (*amor Dei infundens et creans bonitatem in rebus*).[28] Creation, from this point of view, is the communication of the divine joy in the existence of what is other. It is sheer gift. The supreme Good is diffusive of itself (*Bonum est diffusivum sui*). The universe is not a necessary emanation from a transcendent divine source, nor a fulfillment of the being of God, nor is the creativity of God exhausted in the creation angels[29] and the human. Rather, in all its variety and interconnectedness, the created universe is a communication from the heart of God. As the encyclical has it,

> The universe unfolds in God, who fills it completely. Hence, there is a mystical meaning to be found in a leaf,

128

in a mountain trail, in a dewdrop, in a poor person's face. The ideal is…also to discover God in all things. Saint Bonaventure teaches us that "contemplation deepens the more we feel the working of God's grace within our hearts, and the better we learn to encounter God in creatures outside ourselves." (*LS* 233)

It may be the wisest thing to stop here, pondering Pope Francis's words, "At the end, we will find ourselves face to face with the infinite beauty of God (cf. 1 *Cor* 13:12), and be able to read with admiration and happiness the mystery of the universe, which with us will share in unending plenitude" (*LS* 243). Further speculation on the presence of lions and lambs, kangaroos and crocodiles, to say nothing of mosquitos and viruses seems vain, and likely to distract and trivialize the range of hope.[30] Nevertheless, in specifically ecological terms and their relational connotations, the words of *Laudato Si'* are helpfully evocative: "Eternal life will be a shared experience of awe, in which each creature, resplendently transfigured, will take its rightful place" (*LS* 243). In other words, God does not consign to annihilation—even if that were possible—the world that the divine love and beauty has created.

THE CHRISTIC ECONOMY

The elaboration of a theology refocused on eschatological and ecological dimensions of incarnational economy is a daunting task, as previously noted. The concrete conditions and dimensions of God's "all in all" communication are given only in the *via negativa* of hope and in the open-endedness of its connotation. Any possible application to the whole terrestrial world of "animal, vegetable, and mineral" in relation to the transformed Body of Christ, Head and members, remains speculative. Even regarding the human being as a member of Christ, an eschatological reserve is required: "Beloved, we are God's children now; what we will be has not yet been revealed. What we do know is this: when he is revealed, we will be like him, for we will see him as he is" (1 John 3:2). Ultimate hope in all its possible forms of fulfillment outstrips theory, imagination, and prediction. Still, the life of faith has its own sensibility and connatural sense of reality, as hope unfolds within a field of embodied communication, centered in the crucified and risen Christ, and reaching out to all things in him.

The rejection of an anthropocentric outlook must not obscure the fact that the only way for the universe to be known to us human beings is through the human mind and heart. That does not mean that everything is reducible to human fulfillment, but it does mean that the human mind remains and grows ever more open to the expanse of the universe. "The soul is in some sense all things" (*anima est quodammodo omnia*), as expressed by Aquinas following Aristotle.[31] The human is not the end, for that can only be found in the infinite being and goodness of God. Nevertheless, the knowledge of the universe and its glories relies on the potential of human intelligence to be open to a limitless domain of being.

Though a notion of the universe presupposes the potential outreach of human intelligence, the fulfillment of what is so known exceeds the mere fact of its becoming an object of human knowledge. The eschatological fulfillment ("God all in all") is determined by the Creator, the beginning and the end. From a Christian perspective, this end is not in an abstractly generic eschatological fulfillment. Rather, it is concrete, particular, and in every detail "christic" from the beginning, for Christ "is before all things, and in him all things hold together" (Col 1:17).

When Christ is considered as the Word through whom all things came into being (John 1:2), theocentric, christocentric, and even anthropocentric horizons fuse and converge at the same point, and open out to the inclusive novelty of a new heaven and a new earth. In that respect, it might be feared that this christic, cosmic, and universal horizon is merely a glorified anthropocentricity. An anthropocentric reduction of eschatology and divine creativity and generosity simply to the fulfillment of the human abstracted from other elements in the terrestrial environment is a distortion. There are at least two points that must be considered: First, it is imperative to appreciate the particular—and the as yet unknown—economy of God's creative and redemptive action. Therefore, rather than employing narrowly anthropocentric terms, it is essential to keep in mind a horizon determined only by God's self-revelation and grace. That would include the primordial self-giving of God in Christ, the vocation of the human within all creation, and the ultimate glorification of God "all in all." Consequently, human fulfillment would be necessarily centered in a christic and cosmic context.

Second, the human along with all creation must be appreciated "in Christ." The incarnation, as an expanding event, must be set within the continuing economy of God's self-communication. Christ is still incarnate—still being incarnated—just as we are already members of his paschal Body. The cosmic scope of the incarnation has been too long tabernacled in an interiority lacking a sense of the corporate and cosmic relationships involved. The character of eschatological environment cannot be considered apart from the dynamic of participation in the Body of Christ—and in the cosmic and communitarian dimensions of the new creation.

It might be that a satisfactory answer will be beyond the epistemic capabilities and imagination of our age. There may be some perceptions of the Body of Christ and the scope of the incarnation reserved only to those who are fully transformed into him. The rest of us on this pilgrimage of time must remain alert to the points of convergence of many aspects of faith if we are not to downplay the eschatological inclusiveness of Christ in relation to the whole of the universe:

- The Word was incarnate on this earth.
- As the risen Lord, in his body he is the firstfruits of the world transformed.
- He already fills the universe in his presence and power.
- He is not so much an individual in the world, but the one in whom the world exists in its eschatological plenitude.
- The Eucharist forms the Body of the Church as the dwelling place of God.[32]

The Chalcedonian dogma is quite clear. In the incarnation, the Word is hypostatically united to a human nature. But that is not to restrict Christ exclusively to the human. There is still the universe to be considered—which was not the concern of Chalcedon. God was in Christ reconciling *the world* to himself (2 Cor 5:19), originally and finally inclusive of all that constitutes that world. Though Christ is not hypostatically united to each element of creation, the whole of creation nonetheless finds its consistency, coherence, and finality in him. It would seem, then, that the Word's personal hypostatic union with a human nature is so constituted as to bring home to human consciousness the entirely christic character of the universe. That, in turn, suggests to Christian hope that the ultimate milieu is characterized by a living system of interrelationships, interdependence, interaction, and communion. Certainly, the gift of eternal life means life to the full (see John 10:10). In this respect, essential considerations are seeing God "face to face," union with the risen Christ, the consequent resurrection of the body, and communion with all in the Spirit of love and unity. Is there more to be added? To put it another way, would eternal life be truly life to the full, life in its most abundant form, if it meant life without the world of our embodiment in which the Word became flesh? Can the glorified Body of Christ, head and members, be intelligible without a glorified and transformed world? While allowing for unimaginable transformations in terms of the creative power of God, and God's becoming "all in all" in a primordial self-sacrificial love, some questions stir. Is it appropriate to the divine power and love to think of this animal, vegetable, and mineral world, without its being restored, transfigured, and transformed in the ultimate moment of God's self-communication? After all, Christ rose in the body—and, for the Catholic faith, Mary is assumed into heaven (as presented more fully in the preceding chapter). With the solemn declaration of the dogma of the assumption in 1950, the intentionality of faith has hurried past its powers of expression. If Mary is declared to be assumed, body and soul, into heaven, the authority of the Catholic Church is thereby committed to a view of materiality, corporeality, and physicality that is as yet beyond our powers of expression. Nonetheless, in the confession of both the resurrection of the Crucified and the assumption of Mary, we are already affirming the boundless love and creativity of God. Little more can be said, unless to express wonder and reverent questioning. The details must be left to the God who has creatively loved our world, and everything in it, into existence, more than is possible for any human love as was mentioned earlier.

A venerable theological axiom states, "Grace heals, perfects, and elevates nature." However, no perfect symmetry is implied between our present understanding of nature, its ecology and environment, on the one hand, and the new creation in which God is all in all (1 Cor 15:28), on the other. The gift of God never fits neatly into a human system of anticipation and expectation. The shock of the cross and the surprise of the resurrection are always too much for the expectations of human wisdom (see 1 Cor 1:25). Hope needs to live in another sense of proportion, determined only by the incalculable generosity of God, while being focused in him who is "the Alpha and the Omega, the first and the last, the beginning and the end" (Rev 22:13). While the self-giving and transforming love of God is already at work, the end will come in God's time and on God's terms. Then, the creative Spirit will breathe the fragmented vocabulary of our present existence into the great poem of the new creation. Admittedly, the form of God's ultimate creative act defies both thought and imagination, hope is justified in envisaging an eschatological milieu in which the glory of God will be made manifest in every detail of creation.

CONCLUSION

The foregoing reflection has been little more than an elaboration of an all-inclusive hope in the spirit of *Laudato Si'*. Hope for a new creation in Christ includes the liberation and transformation of earthly nature when God will be "all in all" (1 Cor 15:28). Biblical perspectives regarding the city of God (Rev 21:2), and the Lamb slain "from the foundation of the world" (Rev 13:8, etc.), despite the tragedies and violence of the ecological world, extend the range and concreteness of this hope.

The God-intended multiplicity of creation and the primordial creativity of love itself are grounds for a reconsideration of the future of the natural world, and what hope in "the resurrection of the body" might entail. In this regard, the focus remains incarnational: not only did the Word become flesh, but it also became an "earthling" in a planetary environment. Without sentimental, trivial, or anxious projections of the details of what the fulfillment of all creation in God might mean, a soberly critical hope is justified in suggesting that the world of nature and its life-forms will not be simply left behind. Relying on the creative, self-giving love of God, hope can anticipate a final evidence of how "nature is never spent," and finally recognize "the dearest freshness deep down things,"[33] in that fullness of life animating the world to come.

CHAPTER 8

An Open-Ended Ecology

THE PRECEDING CHAPTERS are designed to further the theory and practice of integral ecology. They have depended on prior, fertile philosophical and theological traditions, which, in turn, stand to be enriched by a more ecological outlook. This chapter presents two examples: the first deals with what an integral ecology might inherit from natural law tradition; and the second, the continuing relevance of a sacramental and Eucharistic vision.

But first, a summary of what has been presented so far:

Chapter 1 introduced more fully the notion of an *integral* ecology. Building on my previous investigations into *Laudato Si': On Care for Our Common Home*, we have taken a step further, and focused on what is entailed in an "integral ecology"—within a cosmopolis of ecological concern.[1] Integral ecology cannot be realized by excluding ideologically any domain or dimension of knowledge from consideration. Therefore, it envisages, however imperfectly, not only particular ecological niches, or even larger habitats, but the whole terrestrial biosphere: in short, the incomprehensible totality of existence in life,[2] received as a gift of "a sublime communion" (*LS* 89). This implies the presence of the giver, and the contemplation of what Christians hold to be the apex of divine giving—the incarnation of Jesus Christ: God so loved the world so as to give his only begotten son (John 3:16). A religious sense of creation provides a background theme in which all our diverse human creativities can improvise their variations within the symphony of reality.

Chapter 2 addressed the question of "Contexts," and first considered "the larger story" that various ecological perspectives may or may not share. However, the very fact that we are *earthlings*—existing and coexisting within this universe—surely suggests that we do have something in common, and that collaboration for the well-being of the planet has become urgently desirable. Hence, the value in continuing to explore some version of a common story of origins becomes clear. Cosmology speaks of an original event of the Big Bang that occurred some 13.8 billion years ago, and a cosmos that is still expanding. The only way to understand what is happening is to participate in its unfolding—so to feel what an integral ecology demands.

The shared narrative structure of experience led inevitably to a consideration of a "new paradigm" for the ecological exploration of reality so that the much lamented "silo" organization of our understanding of the world could give place to more communicative and integrated forms. We touched on the meaning of a "New Age" of human awareness more hospitable to a deeper search for meaning and a desire to learn by heart the movement and form of the interconnected universe in which we so uncannily exist.

Chapter 3, "Ecological Conduct," presented an integral ecology as the process of becoming *someone* in mind, heart, and imagination, and doing *something* in action, as a participant in a global conversion. Here, we consider the value of various kinds of action, along with the role of the higher form of action that is contemplation, a mindful and heartfelt indwelling of the world. What does this mean for the language of our communication, and even the meaning of our humanity, with its unique capacity to ask the big questions arising from the world we live in, the universe in which we participate, and the specific calling and capacity of the human? Here, we touch on the "inner ecology" of human consciousness as integral to the health of biophysical ecology of terrestrial life.

Chapter 4, "Indwelling Creation," explored the realities of the Creator, creation, and ecology from the perspective of human consciousness, the better to interiorize our sense of the presence of God and to extend the possibility of dialogue on many fronts. Such an approach moves "from the inside out," so to speak, with the emphasis on experience, the phenomenon of consciousness and intentionality. As noted, this contrasts with the "from the outside in" perspective with its concern for the purely objective, but without an explicit focus on the interiority of the personal subject. An integral approach cannot neglect the data of consciousness that enable human consciousness, science, ecology, and the life of the spirit to be examined in a more ample and integrated fashion—in the interests of any integral ecology.

In chapter 5, "Christ and Integral Ecology," we noted that for an integral ecology, the meaning of the incarnation is crucial, but understood as an expanding event. The resurrection and ascension of Christ do not mean that he has become disincarnate and disembodied, but, rather, that he is fully embodied in the world as it will be. It is not that the risen Christ is now disembodied, but that, as human beings, we are not yet fully embodied in a transformed creation. The incarnation continues, and the world in which the Word was made flesh reaches an unimaginable fulfillment in Christ. The consequences for an integral ecology were considered in chapter 7.

Chapter 6, "Befriending Death," admitted that there is little room for death in many presentations of ecology, even in *Laudato Si'*. Yet, death is an obvious ecological reality, as generation follows generation. It has been remarked that a primal fear of death motivates much of culture and individual lifestyles. The denial of death has ecological consequences, while the acknowledgment of death calls into question the superficial ecology that is sustained merely by romantic optimism. By reflecting on the ecological significance of death, we can ensure that the framework of integral ecology is realistic and truly open to the witness of Christian faith and hope as it brings a special depth and hope into ecological concerns.

In chapter 7, "Ecology and Eschatology," we noted how Pope Francis's *Laudato Si'* provokes the need for both ecological and eschatological reflection on how ultimate fulfillment in Christ includes the liberation and transformation of earthly nature. Hope envisages the end when God will be "all in all" (1 Cor 15:28). The biblical perspectives presenting the city of God (Rev 21:2), and the Lamb slain from the foundation of the world (Rev 13:8) extend the range and concreteness of hope, along with a deeper appreciation of both the God-willed multiplicity of creation and the primordial creativity of love itself. With this incarnational focus, the Word not only became flesh but also is an "earthling" in a particular planetary environment. Consequently, eschatological fulfillment does not entail the abolition of the natural world, but its unimaginable fulfillment.

This chapter deals with the ever-widening horizon implicit in "toward an integral ecology" as it incorporates the philosophical tradition of natural law and the liturgical and religious perspectives of eucharistic sacramentality.

NATURAL LAW AND INTEGRAL ECOLOGY

If we speak in a language that might help a worldwide ecological conversation, participants cannot be too theological or limited to the terms of a specific philosophy or culture or language group. While there are rich resources in the natural law tradition, these need to be critically transposed in such a way as to meet the ecological concerns of the entire world in all its variety. Here, the language of natural law based on common reason is a resource. It is not waiting on everyone to become religiously committed or scientifically expert or politically partisan. Reason demands dialogue, and dialogue makes possible an integral ecology. We may not expect that St. Paul would have much time for integral ecology, but he does appeal to the world of common values: "Whatever is true, whatever is honorable, whatever is just, whatever is pure, whatever is pleasing, whatever is commendable, if there is any excellence and if there is anything worthy of praise, think about these things" (Phil 4:8). For Paul, as for all thinkers on ethics, there is a moral imperative inherent in being a member of the human race. Whatever the problems and conflicts that arise, the sense of a shared natural law contributes to the ecology of the common good of life on this planet.

Natural law presupposes some notion of nature as the field of communication in which we identify one another as human in the commonwealth of life on earth, and so wish to collaborate in supporting and enhancing our common terrestrial humanity. In this respect, our humanity is a given, a datum—what each of us is born with. But it is also a program—what we make of ourselves within the world of nature, and "mean the world" to one another, given the wondrous variety of life on earth.

In the global context, it is not enough to repeat the worn-out metaphor of the "global village" with its suggestion that a privileged minority of the world's people consume most of its produce, own most of the natural resources, and control the means of production. In its best connotation, the global context connotes a newly emerging stage in world history. Despite the differences and divisions inherited from the past—in relation to different geographical locations, nations, languages, cultures, and religions—a new consciousness is emerging that, in turn, demands the development of a genuinely integral ecology and planetary responsibility.

In today's historical experience, the sense of our common human emergence is accompanied by new human capacities. The astonishing developments in electronic communications have brought a new intensity and immediacy into human contact and more intentional connection with this planet's varied life-forms. The individual is, in principle, newly embodied in an electronic network of enormous potential for ecological interactions and communication within the emerging world. From this perspective, human nature is less a philosophical abstraction and more something being formed in the creativity of a living communication.

For its part, human intelligence and freedom can be understood as a dimension of the creativity and adaptability of nature in sustaining life in all its forms. The conflicts and problems that arise point to the need for an inner ecology of values to form human consciousness in responsible care within, and for, the biophysical reality of the environment. In that sense, the environmental crisis is not unrelated to the ecology of human culture and its ability to respect a hierarchy of values—physical, biological, vital (health), political, economic, cultural, and religious—in their dynamic confluence within the global good. Natural law and integral ecology converge.

There is the further question of our evolutionary emergence as it affects the notion of natural law. If we become too "spiritual," we may become oblivious to the generic "animality" of the human condition. Our kinship with the animal realm offsets an ethereal sentiment of both individual existence and global belonging, yet unaware of the inherent limitations of each. Feelings and actual bonding are "given" in ways that demand to be respected. Neither interpersonal relations nor religiously inspired universal love can afford to bypass a natural ordering of relationships—as Stephen Pope has convincingly shown.[3] By owning our place in an evolutionary biological world, we are less inclined to think of the human self as a free-floating consciousness. Our present responsibilities have a biologically based emotional constitution. They are shaped in a direction by the genesis of nature. There are "givens" in the human constitution; and these conditions precede freedom, never to be repudiated unless at the cost of denaturing ourselves in a fundamental manner. In sexuality, for instance, neither culture nor a person-centered spirituality is the only consideration. Primary relationships to family, friends, community, society, and to the earth itself need to be recognized in their particularity as priorities in our concerns. We belong to the whole human family through a specific family. We enter the global community by being connected to a special place and time. We are human by being earthlings.

In an integral ecology, natural law is not an abstract law of reason, but rather arises out of embodiment in the world of nature. Thus, human nature is realized by living in communion with the whole of earthly nature, and exercises its intelligence and responsibility in the service of such a "sublime communion" (*LS* 89).

SACRAMENTAL AND EUCHARISTIC

The Eucharist is a primary symbol within the life of Christian faith. Eighteen hundred years ago, St. Irenaeus of Lyons dealt with Gnosticism, the heady "New Age" spirituality of his day. He laid down a basic rule for every age of the Church: "Our way of thinking is attuned to the Eucharist; and the Eucharist in turn confirms our way of thinking."[4] This axiom has ecological consequences when the Eucharist is celebrated as "the summit and source" of the communal life of the Church. It offers, thereby, an inexhaustible surplus of meaning as it brings together what is too often kept apart—the presence of the convivial God, the reality of the incarnation, communion with one another and all living things on this planet, and the cosmos itself. The Eucharist brims with significance as it holds the meaning of nature and culture together in relation to God, Christ, and all creation.

The Eucharist expresses the scope of integral ecology by bringing nature and culture together in the celebration of faith. The "real presence" of the whole Christ is communicated through the transformation of the shared "fruit of the earth and the work of human hands," so that earthly elements sustaining human life and communication are integrated into the "ecology" of God's self-giving in Christ. In this respect, the Eucharist brings together many gifts and many forms of giving. It offers to all who would receive it a "holy communion" within a universe of grace and giving. From nature's giving, there are the grain and the grapes. From the gifts of human work and skill, we have the bread and wine to be offered. From the generous giving of family and friends flow the gifts of good meals and festive celebrations. From Jesus's self-giving at the Last Supper, the disciples were given his "body and blood," food and drink to nourish life in him. He will breathe into the disciples the gift of his Spirit. Working in and through all these gifts and all these modes of giving is the gift of the Father who so loved the world. As the Church celebrates the Eucharist, all these gifts come together to nourish earthly lives with the gift of communion with God. We become, in this world and on this earth, life-givers, love-givers, care-givers.

The Eucharist inspires a vision of the world as a wave of communication—a great field of relationships involving everything and everyone. Even if we human beings have been busy through our brief history in sundering our relationships to our fellow creatures and to the earth itself, the Eucharist suggests an ecological vocation for human beings arising out of faith itself. The most intense moment of communion with God is at the same time an intense moment of our communion with the earth. For "the fruits of the earth and the works of human hands'" are not magically vaporized by the action of the Spirit but come fully into their own ultimate reality. In the idiom of John's Gospel, the bread and wine become "*true* food and *true* drink" (John 6:55, au. emphasis). "Transubstantiated" in this way, the Eucharist anticipates the cosmic transformation that is afoot, not leaving the earth and created cosmos behind, but promising healing and transformation.

In terms of ecological conversion, the ever-renewable resources of faith, hope, and love work to inspire the self-dispossession necessary for conserving the nonrenewable resources and protecting the threatened ecology of our planet. A eucharistic outlook goes beyond a naïve nostalgia for an idealized past, unspoiled and largely unpopulated. Likewise, it counters the doctrinaire evolutionism that tends to empty the significance of the present into an impersonal and incalculable future—with the result that the past and the present have value only in terms of what they are evolving into. The Eucharist provides a more generous perspective. It envisions the God-given future occurring within our earthly and historical time. The meaning of our present existence is not deferred to a future indifferent to what we now are. Our earth, our flesh and blood, *do* matter. We are not being emptied of what we are. For we are fed with the bread of heaven and filled with the energies of the Spirit in the flesh and blood, and in the food and drink, of our present existence. In this hopeful vision, the Body of Christ becomes the milieu of our existence, in which nothing is left out and nothing left behind.

Divine providence has guided the great cosmic processes over billions of years to create the conditions in which planet Earth could be a biosphere, a place of life. The same providence has worked through the evolutionary dynamics that have made us what we are—"earthlings," human beings, coexisting with a million other forms of life in the delicate ecology of this planet. In a continuing chain of giving and receiving, we live not only *with*, but *from* and *off* one another. Capping the long history of gifts, the creative providence of God has led to the incarnation of the Word, so that we might have "life, and have it abundantly" (John 10:10).

The eucharistic command of the Lord, "Do this in memory of me," comes from one who gave himself unreservedly for all. By entering his spirit, we begin to have a heart for all God's creation in its every aspect, that good creation that the Creator has loved into being. By entering Christ's imagination and becoming members of his Body, we are in fact putting our souls back into our bodies, so to be re-embodied in him who is related to everything and everyone, and so to coexist with all creation. We begin to live in a new timeframe determined by the patient, creative goodness of God, who is working to draw all things to their fulfillment.

An Open-Ended Ecology

The eucharistic imagination stimulates new ecological perspectives. Everything has its part in God's creation. Everything has been owned by the Divine Word in the incarnation. Everything is involved in the great transformation already begun in his resurrection. We are bound together in a giving universe, at the heart of which is the self-giving love of God. We are living and dying into an ever-larger selfhood to be realized in a network of relationships pulsing through the universe, and flowing from the trinitarian relationships that constitute the very being of God.

A eucharistic integral ecology welcomes the great, generative reality of the cosmos and the ecological reality of our planetary biosphere. The earth and the universe have their place in the Father's house of "many dwelling places" (John 14:2). To obey Jesus's command, "Do this in memory of me," implies a re-membering of all that has been dismembered in the sterile culture of today's world. In the eucharistic perspective, loving our neighbor means loving the whole cosmic and planetary neighborhood in which all exist. We are enabled, not only to be jubilant participants in the feast, but also, through all the giving and service that life and love demand, destined to be part of the meal, to contribute the energies of our lives to the great banquet of the new creation: "Unless a grain of wheat falls into the earth and dies, it remains just a single grain; but if it dies, it bears much fruit" (John 12:24). With Jesus, we fall as grains of wheat into the holy ground to die, in order not to remain alone.

The Eucharist works as a cure for cosmic solipsism. It sustains a relational existence at odds with any self-enclosed individualistic vision. Jesus prays "that they may all be one. As you, Father, are in me and I am in you, may they also be in us....I in them and you in me, that they may become completely one" (John 17:21–23). Our unity in God derives from the way the Father and the Son are united in the one divine life: the divine persons are not independent entities somehow managing to come together. Divine life is an eternal flow of one into the other, in relationships of mutual self-giving—*perichoresis*: "Instead of taking as the norm of Reality those things which are *outside* one another, he [Jesus] takes as a standard and paradigm those who are *in* one another."[5] Thus, we are challenged to imagine our interrelationships in terms of mutual indwelling modelled on the union existing between the

Father and the Son. We each exist by enabling the other to be—so that the life-giving nourishment we give is not less than the gift of ourselves. We are *in* one another for the life of each other. By being *from* the other, *for* the other, and so, *in* the other, our earthly human lives participate in God's own trinitarian love-life, while being at the same time embodied in the earth itself.

Christian faith moves through time, but always walks on holy ground. The challenge remains: to bring to life an integral ecology respecting the whole of life and the earth itself as the very body of our being together.

In conclusion, as the source and summit of the life of the Church, the Eucharist relates us to Christ, connects us with one another, and continually re-embodies believers within the life of planet Earth. This sacrament is celebrated within a field of transcendent, communal, planetary, and cosmic belonging—as our universe is being drawn into the trinitarian life, toward that ultimate point at which "God will be all in all" (1 Cor 15:28).

Just as despair is fundamentally a failure of imagination, sincere hope is formed in those who have the humility to recognize this earth as the shared body of our existence. Such imagination grows in courage when it is prepared to diagnose the harm caused by the human refusal of this earthly status. More positively, creativity is freshly inspired to the degree we give ourselves to a more intimate collaboration with the gracious mystery of life, however it has been revealed to us. In ecological terms, we are being invited into an embodied awareness in the interconnected, multiform life of the planet itself. The human person is newly perceived as an "earthling" in the great temporal and spatial genesis of the cosmos itself.

This is to say that a new sense of self is being born, characterized by a humility that accepts dependence on a world of living and nonliving things for its existence, nourishment, and delight.

The path to a genuinely integral ecology is always "toward" and remains ever unfinished, capable of moving beyond scientific disagreements, ideological conflicts, and political differences for the sake of the present and ultimate well-being of all who rejoice in the beauty, wonder, and promise of this earthly life.

Notes

INTRODUCTION

1. Anthony J. Kelly, *Laudato Si': Integral Ecology and the Catholic Vision* (Adelaide, South Australia: ATF, 2016).

2. See Claude Romano, *At the Heart of Reason*, trans. Michael Smith and Claude Romano (Evanston, IL: Northwestern University Press, 2016).

3. Gabriel Gomes, *Song of the Skylark I–II: Foundations of Experiential Religion* (Lanham, MD: University of America Press, 1991), 233–48.

CHAPTER 1:
TOWARD AN INTEGRAL ECOLOGY

1. On the notion of cosmopolis, see Bernard Lonergan, *Insight: A Study of Human Understanding* (London: Longmans, Green and Co., 1957), 238–42.

2. Lonergan, *Insight*, 238.

3. Anthony J. Kelly, "The Global Significance of Natural Law: Opportunities, Quandaries and Directions," http://www.acu.edu.au/__data/assets/pdf_file/0004/107527/Kelly_Natural_Law.pdf (accessed September 5, 2017).

4. Claude Romano, *At the Heart of Reason*, trans. Michael Smith and Claude Romano (Evanston, IL: Northwestern University Press, 2016); see, too, for both content and method, Bruno Latour, *Inquiry into Modes of Existence: Anthropology for Moderns* (Cambridge, MA: Harvard University Press, 2011). See also Brendan Purcell, *From Big Bang to Big Mystery:*

Human Origins in the Light of Creation and Evolution (Hyde Park, NY: New City Press, 2011).

5. Michael Polanyi, "Faith and Reason," *Journal of Religion* 41, no. 4 (October 1961): 244. For a fuller treatment, see his *Personal Knowledge* (Chicago: University of Chicago Press, 1958).

6. Denis Edwards, *Jesus and the Cosmos* (Mahwah, NJ: Paulist Press, 1991), 44–54. From a philosophical point of view, see the outstanding Mark Wynn, *God and Goodness: A Natural Theological Perspective* (London: Routledge, 1999).

7. Latour, *Inquiry into Modes of Existence.* See http://www.modesofexistence.org/.

8. See Latour, *Inquiry into Modes of Existence*, 6–10.

9. Anthony Kelly, *An Expanding Theology: Faith in a World of Connections* (Melbourne: E. J. Dwyer, 1993).

10. Bernard Lonergan, *Method in Theology* (Toronto: University of Toronto Press, 2017).

11. Elizabeth Johnson, *Ask the Beasts: Darwin and the God of Love* (New York: Bloomsbury, 2014), 189–93, 230–31.

12. For the full import of such a phrase, see David Tracy, *The Analogical Imagination: Christian Theology and the Culture of Pluralism* (New York: Crossroad, 1981).

13. Aristotle, *De Anima*, 111, 8.

14. Niels Bohr, for instance: "If anybody says he can think about quantum physics without getting giddy, that only shows he has not understood the first thing about them." For this and similar remarks by Richard Feynman, Albert Einstein, and Wolfgang Pauli, see Christopher F. Mooney, "Theology and Science: A New Commitment to Dialogue," *Theological Studies* 52, no. 2 (June 1992): 398–405.

15. Murray Bookchin, *The Philosophy of Social Ecology: Essays on Dialectical Naturalism* (New York: Black Rose Books, 1990), 10.

16. Lonergan, *Method in Theology*, 107, 115.

17. These will range all the way from the great "paradigm shifters" such as Teilhard de Chardin, Bernard Lonergan, and Karl Rahner, to such gifted communicators as Thomas Berry, David Toolan, Sean McDonagh, and Denis Edwards, right through to vigorous popularizers such as Matthew Fox.

18. J. Ronald Engel, "The Ethics of Sustainable Development," in *Ethics of Environment and Development*, ed. J. Ronald Engel and Joan Gibb Engel (Tucson: University of Arizona Press, 1989), 13–15. See also James A. Nash, *Loving Nature: Ecological Integrity and Christian Responsibility* (Nashville, TN: Abingdon Press, 1991), which is especially valuable in the section "The Ecological Complaint against Christianity," 68–91.

19. David Toolan, "'Nature Is a Heraclitean Fire': Reflections on Cosmology in an Ecological Age," *Studies in the Spirituality of the Jesuits* 23, no. 5 (November 1991).

20. Barbara Ward, "Justice in a Human Environment," *IDOC International* 53 (May 1973): 36.

21. For an interesting attempt to set new perceptions into a larger tradition of philosophy, see Laura Landen, "A Thomistic Analysis of the Gala Hypothesis: How New Is This New Look at Life on Earth?" *The Thomist: A Speculative Quarterly Review* 56, no. 1 (1992): 1–17.

22. For the changing situation, see Roger Gottlieb, ed., *The Oxford Handbook of Religion and Ecology* (New York: Oxford University Press, 2006).

23. Simone Weil, *Waiting for God* (London: Fontana, 1959), 116.

24. For a long-term view, Sean McDonagh, *Greening the Christian Millennium* (Dublin: Dominican Publications, 1999).

25. E. F. Schumacher, *A Guide for the Perplexed* (New York: Harper & Row, 1977), 139–40.

CHAPTER 2: CONTEXTS

1. Claude Romano, *L'événement et le monde. Épithée. Essais Philosophiques* (Paris: Presses Universitaires de France, 1998), 60–69; *There Is: The Event and the Finitude of Appearing*, trans. Michael B. Smith (New York: Fordham University Press, 2016), 149–76.

2. Romano, *L'événement et le monde*, 72–96.

3. For extensive treatment of this "new story," see Thomas Berry, *The Dream of the Earth* (San Francisco: Sierra Club Books, 1988); and, more imaginatively, Brian Swimme, *The Universe Is a Green Dragon: A Cosmic Creation Story* (Santa Fe, NM: Bear and Co., 1984).

4. J. Matthew Ashley, "Reading the Universe Story Theologically: Some Critical Questions and a Paradigm," *Theological Studies* 71, no. 4 (December 2010): 870–902.

5. I owe this example originally to a Greenpeace publication.

6. Berry, *The Dream*, 134–35.

7. Thomas Aquinas, *STh.*, I, q. 1, a. 6; II–II, q. 45, a. 3.

8. *STh.*, II–II, q. 45, a. 2.

9. Fritjof Capra and David Steindl-Rast with Thomas Matus, *Belonging to the Universe: Explorations on the Frontiers of Science and Spirituality* (New York: Harper SanFrancisco, 1991).

10. For abundant illuminating material on the rise of human consciousness, see Ken Wilber, *Up from Eden: A Transpersonal View of Human Evolution* (Boulder, CO: Shambhala, 1983). On some aspects of a new paradigm, William Irving Thompson, ed., *Gaia: A Way of Knowing; Political Implications of the New Biology* (Hudson: Lindesfarne Press, 1987).

11. For a fuller exposition of a new paradigm, Fritjof Capra, *The Tao of Physics* (London: Flamingo, 1985); and *The Turning Point: Science, Society and the Rising Culture* (London: Flamingo, 1984).

12. In the collaborative method of theology, there are some eight functional specialties, each with its own distinctive procedures (cf. Bernard Lonergan, *Method in Theology* [Toronto: University of Toronto Press, 2017], 125–45).

13. Denis Edwards, "'Sublime Communion': The Theology of the Natural World in *Laudato Si'*," *Theological Studies* 77, no. 2 (June 2016): 377–91.

14. See Richard Gelwick, *The Way of Discovery: An Introduction to the Thought of Michael Polanyi* (New York: Oxford University Press, 1977), 135–36.

15. The original French title of the monumental work, Jacques Maritain, *The Degrees of Knowledge*, trans. Bernard Wall (London: Geoffrey Bles, 1937).

16. See Lateran IV (1215), in J. Neuner and J. Dupuis, *The Christian Faith* (London: Collins Liturgical Press, 1982), 109.

17. Here I am indebted to Mary Farrell Bednarowski, "Literature of the New Age: A Review of Representative Sources," *Religious Studies Review* 17, no. 3 (July 1991): 209–16.

18. As quoted in Maritain, *The Degrees of Knowledge*, ix.

19. For an especially valuable presentation of the Pauline diagnosis of the human condition, see Brendan Byrne, *Inheriting the Earth: The Pauline Basis for a Spirituality for Our Time* (Sydney: St Pauls Publications, 1990), and "A Pauline Complement to *Laudato Si'*," *Theological Studies* 77, no. 2 (June 2016): 308–28.

20. See R. Sheldrake, *The Rebirth of Nature* (London: Bantam Books, 1992), 49–51.

21. For a critique of the totalitarian attitudes of science, see Bryan Appleyard, *Understanding the Present: Science and the Soul of Modern Man* (London: Picador, 1992); and Mary Midgley, *Science as Salvation: A Modern Myth and Its Meaning* (London: Routledge, 1992).

22. An outstanding resource here is Thomas M. King, *Teilhard de Chardin* (Wilmington, DE: Michael Glazier, 1988), 13–64.

23. Pierre Teilhard de Chardin, *Towards the Future*, trans. Rene Hague (New York: Harcourt Brace Jovanovich, 1975), 209–11.

24. For further details, see King, *Teilhard de Chardin*, 15–19.

25. See my *Trinity of Love: A Theology of the Christian God* (Wilmington, DE: Michael Glazier, 1988), 234–48.

26. David Toolan, *Facing West from California's Shores: A Jesuit's Journey into New Age Consciousness* (New York: Crossroad, 1987), 30.

CHAPTER 3: ECOLOGICAL CONDUCT

1. Reinhard Cardinal Marx, "'Everything Is Connected': On the Relevance of an Integral Understanding of Reality in *Laudato Si'*," *Theological Studies* 77, no. 2 (June 2016): 295–307.

2. See Celia Deane-Drummond, "*Laudato Si'* and the Natural Sciences: An Assessment of Possibilities and Limits," *Theological Studies* 77, no. 2 (June 2016): 392–415.

3. Denis Edwards, *Ecology at the Heart of Faith* (Maryknoll, NY: Orbis, 2006), 182–203.

4. Neil Ormerod, "Renewing the Earth–Renewing Theology," *Pacifica: Australian Theological Studies* 4, no. 3 (Oct 1991): 295–306; and Robert Faricy, *Wind and Sea Obey Him: Approaches to a Theology of Nature* (London: SCM, 1982), 53–61.

5. On the more general aesthetic consideration, Pope John Paul II observes, "*The aesthetic value of creation cannot be overlooked. Our very contact with nature has a deep restorative power; contemplation of its magnificence imparts peace and serenity. The Bible speaks again and again of the goodness and beauty of creation, which is called on to glorify God (cf. Gen 1:4ff; Ps 8:2; 104:1ff; Wis 13: 3–5; Sir 39:16, 33; 43:1, 9)*" (*Peace with God the Creator, Peace with All of Creation* 14).

6. See Sebastian Moore, *The Fire and the Rose Are One* (London: Darton, Longman and Todd, 1980), 5–28.

7. Bernard Lonergan, *Method in Theology* (Toronto: University of Toronto Press, 2017), 103.

8. For an interfaith example, see Francis X. Clooney, *His Hiding Place Is Darkness: A Hindu-Catholic Theopoetics of Divine Absence* (Stanford, CA: Stanford University Press, 2014).

9. Lonergan, *Method*, 105.

10. See Gabriel Gomes, *Song of the Skylark I–II: Foundations of Experiential Religion* (Lanham, MD: University of America Press, 1991).

11. Aquinas, *STh*, II–II, q. 1, a. 2 ad 2. 2.

12. For an evocative intercultural and interfaith approach, see Koo Dong Yun, *The Holy Spirit and Ch'i (QI): A Chiological Approach to Pneumatology* (Eugene, OR: Pickwick, 2012).

13. Thomas F. O'Meara, *Vast Universe: Extraterrestrials and Christian Revelation* (Collegeville, MN: Liturgical Press, 2012).

14. Mary Midgley, *Beast and Man: The Biological Roots of Human Nature* (Ithaca, NY: Cornell University, 1978), 71.

15. Midgley, *Beast and Man*, xiii.

16. See Stephen J. Pope, "The Order of Love and Recent Catholic Ethics: A Constructive Proposal," *Theological Studies* 52, no. 2 (June 1991): 255–88. For a full treatment, see his *Human Evolution and Christian Ethics* (New York: Cambridge University Press, 2007).

CHAPTER 4: INDWELLING CREATION

1. See Stephen M. Barr, *Modern Physics and Ancient Faith* (Notre Dame, IN: University of Notre Dame Press, 2003), 16, 183.

2. Thomas Aquinas, *Sermo V*, in *Dom 2 de Adventu* (Vives XXIX), 194.

3. Note, too, Job's advice: "Ask the animals, and they will teach you; / the birds of the air, and they will tell you; / ask the plants of the earth, and they will teach you; / and the fish of the sea will declare to you. / Who among these does not know / that the hand of the LORD has done this? / In his hand is the life of every living thing / and the breath of every human being" (Job 12:7–10). This text provides a title for Elizabeth Johnson's celebrated book, *Ask the Beasts: Darwin and the God of Love* (New York: Bloomsbury, 2014).

4. Lonergan writes, "Genuine objectivity is the fruit of authentic subjectivity. To seek and employ some alternative prop or crutch invariably leads to some measure of reductionism" (Bernard Lonergan, *Method in Theology* [London: Darton, Longman and Todd, 1972], 292).

5. Thomas Aquinas, *STh* I, q. 88, a. 2, ad 3.

6. Melvin Konner, *The Tangled Wing: Biological Constraints on the Human Spirit* (New York: Harper and Row, 1982), 435.

7. For a challenging treatment of this theme, William Barrett, *Death of the Soul: From Descartes to the Computer* (New York: Doubleday, 1986).

8. Thomas Aquinas, *III Sent.*, d. 29, 1, 3, 3.

9. For an instructive probe into the deep cultural conditions that have affected the question of God, see Neil Ormerod, "In Defence of

Notes

Natural Theology: Bringing God into the Public Realm," *Irish Theological Quarterly* 71 (2007): 227–41.

10. Judith Wright, "Connections," in *Collected Poems (1942 to 1985)* (Sydney: HarperCollins Australia, 2016), 389.

11. Wright, "Five Senses," *Collected Poems (1942 to 1985)*, 174.

12. Robert Faricy, *All Things in Christ* (London: Fount, 1981), 56.

13. Francis S. Collins, *The Language of God: A Scientist Presents Evidence for Belief* (New York: Free Press, 2006).

14. Michael Polanyi, "Faith and Reason," *Journal of Religion* 41, no. 4 (October 1961): 244. For a fuller treatment, see his *Personal Knowledge* (Chicago: University of Chicago Press, 1958).

15. Denis Edwards, *Jesus and the Cosmos* (Mahwah, NJ: Paulist Press, 1991), 44–54. From a philosophical point of view, see the outstanding Mark Wynn, *God and Goodness: A Natural Theological Perspective* (London: Routledge, 1999).

16. Admittedly, this more philosophical understanding does not go back to Genesis, which speaks more of a primal chaos. The *ex nihilo* character of creation was explored more in reaction to later Gnostic and Manichean teachings that supposed a noncreated evil, material principle.

17. See Robert J. Spitzer, *New Proofs for the Existence of God: Contributions of Contemporary Physics and Philosophy* (Grand Rapids: Eerdmans, 2010).

18. Lonergan, *Method*, 341–43.

19. See Thomas Aquinas, *STh*, I, q. 12, a. 13, ad 1: "We are united to God as to one unknown."

20. Alister McGrath, *Dawkin's God: Genes, Memes, and the Meaning of Life* (Oxford: Blackwell, 2005).

21. Werner Heisenberg, "Scientific and religious Truths," in *Quantum Questions*, ed. Ken Wilber (Boston: Shambhala, 1984), 39.

22. Etienne Gilson, "En marge d'un texte," in *Louis de Broglie, Physicien et Penseur* (Paris: Michel, 1953), 153.

23. As an indication of the medieval fascination with science, see Walter Principe, "'The Truth of Human Nature' according to Thomas Aquinas: Theology and Science in Interaction," in *Philosophy and the God of Abraham: Essays in Memory of James A. Weisheipl*, ed. R. James Long (Toronto: Pontifical Institute of Medieval Studies, 1991), 161–77.

24. Wright, "The Forest," in *Collected Poems (1942 to 1985)*, 173.

25. Thomas Aquinas, *STh* I, q. 65, a. 3.

26. Thomas Aquinas, *Summa contra Gentiles* [*ScG*], l. 2, c. 2.

27. *ScG*, l. 2, c. 45.

28. *STh* I, q. 20. a. 2 (author's emphasis).

29. Apart from an abundance of exciting documentation and marvelous instances of the variety of the past, Stephen Jay Gould, *Wonderful Life: The Burgess Shale and the Nature of History* (London: Penguin, 1989) is a striking model of scientific reconstruction, even as it poses profound philosophical questions.

30. Herbert McCabe, *God Matters* (London: Geoffrey Chapman, 1987), 2–9.

31. George Steiner, *Real Presences* (Chicago: University of Chicago Press, 1989).

32. Kathryn Tanner, *God and Creation in Christian Theology: Tyranny or Empowerment?* (Oxford: Basil Blackwell, 1988). This work studies the deep grammar of the classical theological tradition.

33. *ScG*, l. 1, c 25.

34. John Macquarrie, *Principles of Christian Theology* (New York: SCM Press, 1987), 118.

35. *STh* I, q. 8, a. 1.

36. Edwards, *Jesus and the Cosmos*, 53–55. For a different context, see J. Moltmann, *The Way of Jesus Christ* (London: SCM, 1990), 297–301.

37. *ScG* l, 3, c. 69.

38. W. Norris Clarke, "Is Natural Theology Still Viable Today?" in *Prospects for Natural Theology*, ed. E. Long (Washington, DC: Catholic University of America Press, 1992), 181.

39. John Paul II, "Letter to the Reverend George V. Coyne, S.J., Director of the Vatican Observatory," *Origins* 18, no. 23 (November 1988): 378.

CHAPTER 5: CHRIST AND INTEGRAL ECOLOGY

1. Note the two hapax legomena: *theotes* and *somatikos*.

2. For a provocative, stimulating treatment of such questions, see Douglas Farrow, *Ascension Theology* (New York: Continuum, 2011), 33–51.

3. Jean-Luc Marion, *Le phénomène érotique: Six meditations* (Paris: Grasset, 2003), 185. John Paul II's treatment of this point is necessarily more general but still with a strong phenomenological emphasis. See *Theology of the Body: Human Love in the Divine Plan* (Boston, MA: Pauline Books, 1997), 42–63.

4. Marion, *Le phénomène érotique*, 170.

Notes

5. Jean-Luc Marion, *In Excess: Studies of Saturated Phenomena*, trans. Robyn Horner and Vincent Barraud (New York: Fordham University Press, 2002), 100; *Le phénomène érotique*, 170, 180–81.

6. See Paul Gavrilyuk and Sarah Coakley, eds., *The Spiritual Senses: Perceiving God in Western Christianity* (Cambridge: Cambridge University Press, 2012), for an abundance of material—awaiting a full ecological application.

7. Michel Henry, *Incarnation: Une philosophie de la chair* (Paris: Seuil, 2000), 350–52.

8. Hans Urs von Balthasar, *The Glory of the Lord: A Theological Aesthetics*, vol. 7, *Theology: The New Covenant*, trans. Brian McNeil (Edinburgh: T. & T. Clark, 1989), 308–9.

9. Maximus Confessor, *Difficulty* 41:1305B. See Andrew Louth, *Maximus the Confessor* (London: Routledge, 1996), 19–33. I use Louth's translation. See also Lars Thunberg, *Man and the Cosmos: The Vision of St. Maximus the Confessor* (New York: St Vladimir's Seminary, 1985), 132–37. Likewise, Gavrilyuk and Coakley, *The Spiritual Senses*.

10. Pierre Teilhard de Chardin, *Science and Christ*, trans. René Hague (London: Collins, 1965), 13.

11. Cited in Christopher Mooney, *Teilhard de Chardin and the Mystery of Christ* (London: Collins, 1966), 136. While I have been arguing for the unique realism of the Church as the Body of Christ, I am not thereby conceiving of the whole universe as his body, even though he is "head," etc., of all creation. I am leaving open the question of what that universal and cosmic headship entails. I disagree with Farrow and Barth in this area, who see Teilhard as dissolving the personal reality of Jesus into a gnostic Christ figure within an evolutionary ideology. See Farrow, *Ascension Theology*, 54–57.

12. See Douglas Farrow, *Ascension and Ecclesia: On the Significance of the Doctrine of the Ascension for Ecclesiology and Christian Cosmology* (Grand Rapids: Eerdmans, 1999), 263–64; and Hans Urs von Balthasar, *Man in History: A Theological Study* (London: Sheed and Ward, 1972), 287–88.

13. Cf. Anthony J. Kelly and Francis J. Moloney, *Experiencing God in the Gospel of John* (Mahwah, NJ: Paulist Press, 2003), 287–89, and von Balthasar, *Theo-Drama: Theological Dramatic Theory*, vol. 5, *The Last Act*, trans. Graham Harrison (San Francisco, CA: Ignatius Press, 1998), 376–79.

14. Denis Edwards, "'Sublime Communion': The Theology of the Natural World in *Laudato Si'*," *Theological Studies* 77, no. 2 (June 2016): 377–91.

15. See Lohfink, *Die Himmelfahrt Jesu* (Stuttgart, Katholisches Bibelwerk, 1998), especially 279–81.

16. Cf. Hans Urs von Balthasar, *A Theology of History* (London: Sheed and Ward, 1963), 23–77.

17. Von Balthasar, *A Theology of History*, 87.

18. See Hans Urs von Balthasar, *Theo-Logic: Theological Logical Theory*, vol. 3, *The Spirit of Truth*, trans. Graham Harrison (San Francisco, CA: Ignatius Press, 2005), 297–301, for stimulating elaboration of this point.

19. See von Balthasar, *Theo-Drama 5, The Last Act*, 376–79.

20. Regarding Luke's employment of the cloud symbolism, Lohfink remarks, "Die Wolke war bereits fur ihn ein biblisches Symbol, theologische Chiffre fur Dinge, die nur in Bild und Gleichnis anschaulich zu machen sind" (For him, the cloud was already a biblical symbol, a theological cipher for things that can only be visualized in the Image and Likeness). See *Die Himmelfahrt Jesu*, 283. His fine book concludes with a quotation from Maximus of Turin: Sermo XLIV 3 (CChrL XXIII, 179).

21. See Jean-Luc Nancy, *Au fond des images* (Paris: Editions Galilée, 2003).

22. Sergius Bulgakov, *The Lamb of God*, trans. Boris Jakim (Grand Rapids: Eerdmans, 2008), 317–403, esp. 398–99.

23. Bulgakov, *The Lamb of God*, 400.

24. Bulgakov, *The Lamb of God*, 393–98.

25. *De excessu fratris sui*, bk. 1. PL 16, 1354.

26. See Karl Rahner, "The Interpretation of the Dogma of the Assumption," in *Theological Investigations*, trans. C. Ernst (London: Darton, Longman and Todd, 1961), 1:215–27.

CHAPTER 6: BEFRIENDING DEATH

1. Pope John Paul II, *Evangelium Vitae*.

2. There are many references to "integral" describing development, education, and ecology in *Laudato Si'*; see esp. nos. 10, 11, 62, 124, and chaps. 4, 137, 141, 147, 159, 197, 225, 230. The term *integral ecology* first appears in a 2009 document of the International Theological Commission that recognizes the need for the Catholic "natural law" tradition to be open to ecological perspectives—and for these to recognize a fundamental natural law. See "In Search of Universal Ethic: A New Look at the Natural Law," no. 82, http://www.vatican.va/roman_curia/congregations/cfaith/cti_documents/rc_con_cfaith_doc_20090520_legge-naturale_en.html.

3. For an informed and inspiring account, see Denis Edwards, *Ecology at the Heart of Faith* (Maryknoll, NY: Orbis, 2006).

Notes

4. Lucy Bregman, *Death, Dying, Spirituality and Religions: A Study of the Death Awareness Movement* (New York: Peter Lang, 2003) presents a many-faceted movement approaching the phenomenon of death as a meaningful experience beyond the specifically medical context. Her interdisciplinary movement can appear to be purely secular, but, in fact, it tends to draw on the spirituality latent in classic and popular expressions of Judaism, Christianity, and Buddhism—and more besides.

5. Denis Edwards, *Breath of Life: A Theology of the Creator Spirit* (Maryknoll, NY: Orbis, 2004), 137–38, 174.

6. William R. Stoeger, "Scientific Accounts of Ultimate Catastrophes in Our Life-Bearing Universe," in *The End of the World and the Ends of God*, ed. John Polkinghorne and Michael Welker (London: T. & T. Clark, 2000), 19–28, at 21.

7. Stoeger, "Scientific Accounts," 28.

8. Ernest Becker, *The Denial of Death* (New York: The Free Press, 1973), ix.

9. Becker, *The Denial*, 51.

10. Becker, *The Denial*, 51.

11. Becker, *The Denial*, 285.

12. Becker, *The Denial*, 282.

13. Becker, *The Denial*, 282.

14. Becker, *The Denial*, 57.

15. Becker, *The Denial*, 58. See also Andras Angyal, *Neurosis and Treatment: A Holistic Theory* (New York: Wiley, 1965), 260.

16. Hence, the ancient liturgical injunction on Ash Wednesday, as the ashes are traced on the forehead in the sign of the cross: *Memento homo quia pulvus es...*: "Remember, man, thou art but dust...."

17. James Alison, *The Joy of Being Wrong: Original Sin through Easter Eyes* (New York: Crossroad, 1998) is illuminating in this whole area.

18. Alison, *The Joy of Being Wrong*, is a basic reference.

19. Karl Rahner, *On the Theology of Death*, trans. C. H. Henkey (New York: Herder & Herder, 1962), 32–51.

20. See Peter C. Phan, *Eternity in Time: A Study of Karl Rahner's Eschatology* (London: Associated University Press, 1988), 55. See also 53–58 and 207–10.

21. Ladislaus Boros, *The Moment of Truth: Mysterium Mortis*, trans. G. Bainbridge (London: Burns and Oates, 1962).

22. Boros, *The Moment of Truth*, viii. See also 1–23.

23. Boros, *The Moment of Truth*, viii. See also 73–81.

24. Boros, *The Moment of Truth*, viii. See also 73–81.

25. Boros, *The Moment of Truth*, ix.

26. Boros, *The Moment of Truth*, ix, and elaborated in 73–84.

27. See Phan, *Eternity in Time*, 75–115.

28. See Anthony J. Kelly and Francis F. Moloney, *Experiencing God in the Gospel of John* (Mahwah, NJ: Paulist Press, 2003), 270–86.

29. On the empty tomb, see Anthony J. Kelly, *The Resurrection Effect: Transforming Christian Life and Thought* (Maryknoll, NY: Orbis, 2008), 139–45.

30. For elaboration of this point, see Denis Edwards, *Jesus and the Cosmos* (New York: Paulist Press, 1991), 103–32.

31. John Polkinghorne, *Science and Creation: The Search for Understanding* (London: SPCK, 1988), 64–68.

32. Denis Edwards, *Partaking of God: Trinity, Evolution and Ecology* (Collegeville, MN: Liturgical Press, 2014), 88; See also the chapter "Evolution, Cooperation, and the Theology of Original Sin," 130–46.

33. Becker, *The Denial of Death*, 282.

34. See Anthony J. Kelly, *Eschatology and Hope* (Maryknoll, NY: Orbis, 2006), esp. chap. 4, "The Paschal Mystery: The Parable of Hope," 73–95.

35. Ghislain Lafont, *Peut-on connaître Dieu en Jésus-Christ?* (Paris: Éditions du Cerf, 1969), 237–58. For the broader context, see Anne Hunt, *The Trinity and the Paschal Mystery: A Development in Recent Catholic Theology* (Collegeville, MN: Liturgical Press, 1997), chap. 2, "Death and Being, Human and Divine," 37–56. Regarding eschatology, see Hunt, chap. 11, "Trinity and Eschatology," in *The Trinity: Nexus of the Mysteries of Faith* (Maryknoll, NY: Orbis, 2005), 200–216.

CHAPTER 7: ECOLOGY AND ESCHATOLOGY

1. See Richard W. Miller, "Deep Responsibility for the Deep Future," *Theological Studies* 77, no. 2 (June 2016): 436–65.

2. Gerard Manley Hopkins, "God's Grandeur," in *Poems of Gerard Manley Hopkins*, ed. Robert Bridges (London: Humphrey Milford, 1918), 26.

3. On the beatific vision, see Anthony J. Kelly, *Eschatology and Hope* (Maryknoll, NY: Orbis Books, 2006), 166–74.

4. The sentence "something to give those poor men and women who will have been liberated once and for all" is very compressed, yet the meaning is clear if we take the next paragraph (*LS* 244) into consideration.

5. Basil the Great, *Hom. In Hexaemeron*, 1,2, 6 (PG, 29,8.).

Notes

6. For the ecumenical context of ecological concerns, see Anthony J. Kelly, "The Ecumenism of Ecology," *Australian eJournal of Theology* 22, no. 3 (December 2015): 193–204.

7. To inspire energetic hope in the present crisis, see Michael McCarthy, *The Moth Snowstorm: Nature and Joy* (London: Hodder and Stoughton, 2015).

8. For an erudite alternative to our approach, see Paul J. Griffiths, *Decreation: The Last Things of All Creatures* (Waco, TX: Baylor University Press, 2014). This analytically critical and valuable study of matters eschatological seems to lack a metaphysical appreciation of matter and spirit, and to be too wedded to space-time materiality in its treatment of angels and even the possibility of God annihilating what has been created.

9. Peter C. Phan, "Eschatology and Ecology: The Environment in the End-Time," *Irish Theological Quarterly* 62, no. 1 (March 1996): 3–16.

10. Phan, "Eschatology and Ecology," 14–15.

11. See Anthony J. Kelly, "Human Consciousness, God and Creation," *Pacifica* 28, no. 1 (February 2015): 3–22. Cf. also chap. 4, "Indwelling Creation."

12. See, e.g., Eugenio Corsini, *The Apocalypse: The Perennial Revelation of Jesus Christ*, trans. and ed. Francis J. Moloney (Wilmington, DE: Michael Glazier, Inc., 1983); and Craig A. Koester, *Revelation*, Anchor Yale Bible 38A (New Haven, CT: Yale University Press, 2014), 113–206.

13. Anthony J. Kelly, "'The Body of Christ: Amen': The Expanding Incarnation," *Theological Studies* 71, no. 4 (December 2010): 792–816.

14. Hans Urs von Balthasar, *The Glory of the Lord: A Theological Aesthetics*, vol. 7, *Theology: The New Covenant*, trans. Brian McNeil (Edinburgh: T. & T. Clark, 1989), 308–9.

15. E.g., Walter J. Ong, *Orality and Literacy: The Technologizing of the Word*, 2nd ed. (New York: Routledge, 2002).

16. For the gifts of *subtilitas, agilitas,* and *claritas,* see STh Supplementum, qq. 83–85; q. 95 considers these gifts in relation to the risen Christ.

17. Celia Deane-Drummond concludes her monumental work *The Wisdom of the Liminal: Evolution and Other Animals in Human Becoming* (Grand Rapids: Eerdmans, 2014) with the words, "We are caught up *together* in a common society that we can hope will be transformed for the greater glory of God. The glory is certainly humanity fully alive, but it is a life enriched by an interlaced past, present and future with other animals in all their marvellous diversity," 317.

18. Denis Edwards, *Partaking of God: Trinity, Evolution and Ecology* (Collegeville, MN: Liturgical Press), 88. See also the chapter "Evolution, Cooperation, and the Theology of Original Sin," 130–46.

19. For a convincing exegetical and theological argument in favor of preexistence, see Brendan Byrne, "Christ's Pre-existence in Pauline Soteriology," *Theological Studies* 58, no. 2 (May 1997): 308–30.

20. Revelation's presentation of the sheer grace of Jesus's death and resurrection "from before all time," in a way parallel to the Pauline understanding of Jesus as the image of an invisible God (Philippians and Colossians), and the Johannine understanding of the eternal union between God and the Logos, may prove to be a significant contribution to Christian ecological thought.

21. Francis J. Moloney, "The Gospel of Creation: A Biblical Response to *Laudato Si'*," a paper given in October 2015, in Rome, at the ACU-CUA Centre during a conference on "The Greening of the Church."

22. The positively "unknowing" orientation of christocentric and theological hope is preferable to the abstract theorizing. For the complexities involved, see Joshua R. Brotherton, "Presuppositions of Balthasar's Universalist Hope and Maritain's Alternative Eschatological Proposal," *Theological Studies* 76, no. 4 (December 2015): 698–717. See also Michael McClymond, "*Origenes Vindicatus vel Rufinus Redivivus? A Review of Ilaria Ramelli's The Christian Doctrine of Apokatastasis (2013)*," *Theological Studies* 76, no. 4 (December 2015): 813–26.

23. Griffiths, *Decreation*, 282–83; 275–78.

24. Aquinas, *STh* I, q. 47, a. 1.

25. St. Augustine, *Ennar.in Psal.30*, PL 36, 252.

26. *Christic* is a useful alternative to *christocentric*, for it is more open-ended and inclusive in its connotation.

27. Aquinas *STh* I, q. 20. a. 2.

28. Aquinas, *STh* I, q. 20, a.2.

29. The place of angels in creation and in the new creation deserves extensive consideration. A strange amnesia has come upon theology in the modern period in contrast to the creativity of medieval thought. Given the limitations of this present reflection, it might be sufficient to remark that angels witness to dimensions of creation more than the space-time materiality of the present world. Contemporary interest in the possibilities of people meeting their pets in heaven must not be allowed to distract from unimaginable plurality and grandeur of creation represented in the angelic realm. See Griffiths, *Decreation*, 111–51, for a stimulating and somewhat controversial treatment of this topic.

30. For a larger perspective, see Johnson, *Ask the Beasts*, 184–92.

31. Aquinas, *STh* I, q. 16, a.3; q. 84, a.2, ad 2.

32. Mary L. Coloe, *Dwelling in the Household of God: Johannine Ecclesiology and Spirituality* (Collegeville, MN: Liturgical Press, 2007), notes that it is not a matter merely of future existence in a divine realm but of

God dwelling with us in the world, in the great household of faith (see also 1 Pet 3:21–22; Acts 3:21).

33. Gerard Manley Hopkins, "God's Grandeur," in Bridges, *Poems of Gerard Manley Hopkins*, 26.

CHAPTER 8: AN OPEN-ENDED ECOLOGY

1. On the notion of cosmopolis, see Bernard Lonergan, *Insight: A Study of Human Understanding* (London: Longmans, Green and Co., 1957), 238–42.

2. *Laudato Si'*, esp. chap. 4.

3. See Stephen J. Pope, "The Order of Love and Recent Catholic Ethics: A Constructive Proposal," *Theological Studies* 52, no. 2 (June 1991): 255–88. For a full treatment, see Stephen J. Pope, *Human Evolution and Christian Ethics* (New York: Cambridge University Press, 2007).

4. *Adv. Haereses* 4, 18, 5: PG 7/1, 1028.

5. Beatrice Bruteau, "Eucharistic Ecology and Ecological Spirituality," *Cross Currents* 40, no. 4 (Winter 1990–91): 502.

Selected Bibliography

Ashley, J. Matthew. "Reading the Universe Story Theologically: Some Critical Questions and a Paradigm." *Theological Studies* 71, no. 4 (December 2010): 870–902.

Becker, Ernest. *The Denial of Death*. New York: The Free Press, 1973.

Boros, Ladislaus. *The Moment of Truth: Mysterium Mortis*. Translated by G. Bainbridge. London: Burns and Oates, 1962.

Bumbaugh, Julia, and Natalia Imperatori-Lee, eds. *Turning to the Heavens and the Earth: Theological Reflections on a Cosmological Conversion; Essays in Honor of Elizabeth A. Johnson*. Collegeville, MN: Liturgical Press, 2016.

Burrell, David B., and Bernard McGinn, eds. *God and Creation: An Ecumenical Symposium*. Notre Dame, IN: University of Notre Dame Press, 1990.

Byrne, Brendan. "A Pauline Complement to *Laudato Si'*." *Theological Studies* 77, no. 2 (June 2016): 308–28.

Castillo, Daniel P. "Integral Ecology as a Liberationist Concept." *Theological Studies* 77, no. 2 (June 2016): 353–76.

Deane-Drummond, Celia. "*Laudato Si'* and the Natural Sciences: An Assessment of Possibilities and Limits." *Theological Studies* 77, no. 2 (June 2016): 392–415.

Delio, Ilia. *The Unbearable Wholeness of Being: God, Evolution, and the Power of Love*. Maryknoll, NY: Orbis, 2013.

Edwards, Denis. *The Natural World and God: Theological Explorations*. Hindmarsh, South Australia: ATF Press, 2017.

————. "'Sublime Communion': The Theology of the Natural World in *Laudato Si'*." *Theological Studies* 77, no. 2 (June 2016): 377–91.

Gavrilyuk, Paul, and Sarah Coakley, eds. *The Spiritual Senses: Perceiving God in Western Christianity*. Cambridge: Cambridge University Press, 2012.

Gottlieb, Roger, ed. *The Oxford Handbook of Religion and Ecology*. New York: Oxford University Press, 2006.

Hart, David Bentley. *The Experience of God: Being, Consciousness, Bliss*. New Haven, CT: Yale University Press, 2013.

Haught, John F. *Christianity and Science: Toward a Theology of Nature*. Maryknoll, NY: Orbis, 2007.

Heller, Michael. *The New Physics and a New Theology*. Translated by George Coyne et al. Notre Dame, IN: University of Notre Dame Press, 1996.

Hunt, Anne. *The Trinity: Insights from the Mystics*. Collegeville, MN: Liturgical Press, 2010.

————. *Trinity: Nexus of the Mysteries of Trinitarian Faith*. Maryknoll, NY: Orbis, 2005.

Jeanrond, Werner G. *A Theology of Love*. London: T&T Clark, 2010.

Johnson, Elizabeth. *Ask the Beasts: Darwin and the God of Love*. New York: Bloomsbury, 2014.

Kelly, Anthony J. *Eschatology and Hope*. Maryknoll, NY: Orbis, 2006.

————. *Laudato Si': Integral Ecology and the Catholic Vision*. Hindmarsh, SA: ATF, 2016.

————. *The Resurrection Effect: Transforming Christian Life and Thought*. Maryknoll, NY: Orbis, 2008.

————. *Upward: Faith, Church, and the Ascension of Christ*. Collegeville, MN: Liturgical Press, 2014.

Kelly, Anthony J., and Francis F. Moloney. *Experiencing God in the Gospel of John*. Mahwah, NJ: Paulist, 2003.

Latour, Bruno. *Inquiry into Modes of Existence: Anthropology for Moderns*. Cambridge, MA: Harvard University Press, 2011.

Lonergan, Bernard J. F. *Insight: A Study of Human Understanding*. London: Longmans, Green and Co., 1957.

McDonagh, Sean. *Greening the Christian Millennium*. Dublin: Dominican Publications, 1999.

Midgley, Mary. *Animals and Why They Matter*. New York: Penguin, 1983.

Selected Bibliography

———. *Beast and Man: The Biological Roots of Human Nature.* Ithaca, NY: Cornell University Press, 1978.

Moloney, Francis J. *Love in the Gospel of John: An Exegetical, Theological, and Literary Study.* Grand Rapids: Baker Academic, 2013.

O'Meara, Thomas F. *Vast Universe: Extraterrestrials and Christian Revelation.* Collegeville, MN: Liturgical Press, 2012.

Ormerod, Neil. *A Public God: Natural Theology Reconsidered.* Minneapolis, MN: Fortress Press, 2015.

Phan, Peter C. "Eschatology and Ecology: The Environment in the End-Time." *Irish Theological Quarterly* 62, no. 1 (March 1996): 3–16.

Purcell, Brendan. *From Big Bang to Big Mystery: Human Origins in the Light of Creation and Evolution.* Hyde Park, NY: New City Press, 2011.

Romano, Claude. *At the Heart of Reason.* Translated by Michael Smith and Claude Romano. Evanston, IL: Northwestern University Press, 2016.

Tallis, Richard. *Aping Mankind: Neuromania and Darwinitis, and the Misrepresentation of Humanity.* Durham: Acumen, 2011.

Toolan, David. "'Nature Is a Heraclitean Fire': Reflections on Cosmology in an Ecological Age." *Studies in the Spirituality of the Jesuits* 23, no. 5 (November 1991).

Vincie, Catherine. *Worship and the New Cosmology.* Collegeville, MN: Liturgical Press, 2014.

Index of Authors/Names